KU-657-739

Future Publishing Limited
30 Monmouth Street, Bath, BA1 2BW, UK
Telephone +44 (0)1225 442244
Email bookazines@futurenet.com

INTERNATIONAL BOOKAZINES
Editor-in-chief Simon Kirrane
Commercial Manager Liza Austin
Senior Art Editor Lee Caple
Senior Editor Robin Alway
Production Assistant Bridie Roman
Contributors Simon Witton, Marcus Hawkins

For all advertising enquiries
Clare Coleman-Straw
clare.coleman-straw@futurenet.com

LICENSING
International Director Regina Erak
regina.erak@futurenet.com

CIRCULATION
Trade Marketing Manager John Lawton
john.lawton@futurenet.com

PRINT & PRODUCTION
Production Co-ordinator Vivienne Turner
vivienne.turner@futurenet.com
Production Manager Mark Constance
mark.constance@futurenet.com

INTERNATIONAL EXPORT
Head of International Newsstand
Richard Jefferies
richard.jefferies@futurenet.com
International Account Manager
Rebecca Hill
rebecca.hill@futurenet.com

Director of Consumer Revenues
Richard Walker

Imprint
**First published in Great Britain in 2011 by
Dorling Kindersley Limited. 80 Strand,
London WC2R ORL
A Penguin Random House Company
© 2011, 2013 Dorling Kindersley Limited.**

**Content taken from Grow Something to Eat
Everyday, 2011. ISBN 978-1-4153-6227-6**

Future produces high-quality multimedia products which reach our audiences online, on mobile and in print. Future attracts over 50 millions consumers to its brands every month across five core sectors: Technology, Entertainment, Music, Creative and Sports & Auto. We export and license our publications.

Future plc is a public company quoted on the London Stock Exchange (symbol: FUTR).
www.futureplc.com

Chief executive Mark Wood
Non-executive chairman Peter Allen
Chief financial officer Graham Harding
Tel +44 (0)207 042 4000 (London)
Tel +44 (0)1225 442 244 (Bath)

FSC
www.fsc.org
MIX
Paper from responsible sources
FSC® C007184

♻ **recycle**
When you have finished with this magazine please recycle it.

We are committed to only using magazine paper which is derived from well managed, certified forestry and chlorine-free manufacture. Future Publishing and its paper suppliers have been independently certified in accordance with the rules of the FSC (Forest Stewardship Council).

Welcome

More and more people are discovering that the advantages of growing your own fruit and vegetables go far beyond being able to pop outside and pick something to eat. Home-grown produce tastes better than anything in the shops because it's freshly picked and perfectly ripe, which shines through even when cooked or preserved. This complete guide to the gardener's year covers what you'll need to sow, plant, and harvest each month to ensure that your patch remains a source of delicious produce and life all year round.

About the author

Jo Whittingham is a garden writer with a postgraduate degree in horticulture from the University of Reading, and keenly grows her own crops in a plot bursting with produce. Author of Grow Something to Eat Every Day, awarded the Garden Media Guild's Practical Book of the Year 2011, she has also written two books in DK's RHS Simple Steps to Success series; Vegetables and Fruit in Pots and Vegetables in a Small Garden. She also writes for Amateur Gardening magazine and The Scotsman.

Your growing space

You might imagine that you would need ample space to make growing your own fruit and vegetables worthwhile, when in fact even the tiniest sunny corner or windowsill is enough to make a good start. With a little imagination, time, and effort, you can transform almost any space into a productive plot.

Where to grow

The happy truth is that you can grow fruit and vegetables anywhere with reasonable soil, as long as it's not in deep shade all day long. If you're lucky enough to have a large garden, you might consider setting out a dedicated vegetable plot, several fruit trees, and even a cage to protect soft fruit bushes from marauding birds.

Having a smaller garden need not restrict the range of crops you grow, you just need to be more creative in how you use space to fit them in. For instance, you might try filling the vertical space on walls and fences with trained fruit trees and bushes, or plant climbing crops, like peas, beans, and cucumbers. Productive plants can also make attractive additions to your flower borders – don't be afraid to plug summer gaps with fast-growing lettuces, add height to your planting with tall, leafy, sweet corn, or give a neatly pruned redcurrant pride of place.

Containers are another way of turning almost any outside space into a burgeoning edible garden.

It is possible to grow almost any fruit and vegetables in pots on sunny patios, roof terraces and balconies, as long as they are protected from strong winds; and you can keep them well watered and fed. Even small windowboxes and hanging baskets can provide good crops of salads, herbs, and cherry tomatoes, if well cared for.

Try experimenting with crops in pots, from pears to potatoes, French beans to figs, and look out for special dwarf varieties that have been specifically bred to suit cultivation in containers.

(above) **Vertical spaces** allow you to grow more crops in a smaller space. Fruit trees, such as apples, pears and figs can be trained against walls.

(left) **Crops in containers** are the ideal solution if you have limited growing space. Any good-size container with adequate drainage is suitable.

(above) **Sunny windowsills** are warm and bright, and provide a convenient spot to raise young plants for extra early crops.

(right) **Community gardens** offer welcome growing spaces; and are a great way to meet like-minded people to share advice and produce. Ask your council about local schemes in your area.

Plan your plot

Whether you have a generous plot or a tiny postage stamp in which to grow, it is important to plan how you use the space, both to maximize productivity, and to make maintenance easier.

First consider the location of permanent structures – work out if the greenhouse will get enough sunlight, the paths are wide enough, and the compost bins sited in a convenient place.

Once you have decided a layout, think about where you will plant trees, fruit bushes, and perennial vegetables like rhubarb. It's important to put these in the right place first time because they take a few years to establish and start cropping, and will be set back if you have to move them. The great thing about the rest of your vegetable crops is that you grow them afresh each year. Be bold, because any mistakes won't be with you for long.

Alternative spaces

If your own garden doesn't have enough space to fulfil your ambitions, consider taking on an allotment, or investigate local shared community gardens and land-share schemes. These can be great places to learn the ropes, with more experienced gardeners who are usually generous with their advice. They may even organize practical workshops for novice growers.

With the increased popularity of growing your own, there is often considerable demand for a patch to cultivate, so be patient, and be prepared to join a waiting list if necessary.

Where outdoor garden space is limited, don't overlook growing indoors on windowsills, and in glazed porches and conservatories. The light and warmth found here is ideal for raising seedlings and for growing heat-loving plants, such as tomatoes, sweet peppers, chillies, and aubergines, which may struggle outside in a cooler regions. Choose smaller varieties though, so the mature plants don't block too much daylight when fully grown.

Many herbs thrive growing on windowsills, where they are convenient for picking. Seeds can also be sprouted on the kitchen work top at any time of year.

Well planned spaces make growing fruit and vegetables easier and more productive. Take time to work out where permanent features, such as paths and greenhouses, should go.

Using space

Constructing raised beds is one of the best ways of creating growing space where there was none before. As long as the beds themselves are well drained, they can be built on very poor or badly drained soil, or on a patio, then filled with plenty of good topsoil and compost to give good results.

If you have, or are planning, a dedicated kitchen garden, you can make the most of your space by using a bed system, setting up

(right) **Raised beds create instant** growing space on any surface; filled with good-quality soil and compost they can be very productive. Keep them small for easy access and maintenance.

a series of narrow beds separated by access paths. With this system you don't need to allow room for walking on the soil between rows, so you can pack your plants more closely in the growing area for a higher yield.

Flowers, fruit, and veg

Using flower beds to grow crops is a more attractive idea than it might sound. Many vegetables have appealing foliage and flowers, while fruit bushes and trees bear blossom and bright berries that merit a place in any garden. Just be aware that crop plants are more demanding than flowering plants; dig in plenty of manure or compost before planting, and give them ample light and space. Perennial herbs and edible flowers are particularly suitable as border plants, but colourful salads, kales, and Swiss chard can be highly effective, too, especially if you use every scrap of space by intercropping them between ornamentals. Train climbing beans or squashes up decorative supports with spectacular results.

(above left) **An old tin bath** makes an interesting container for this crop of garlic. Ensure that recycled containers have adequate drainage.

(left) **Make the most of your growing** area, whether it is large or small, by planting your crops as closely as practicable in evenly spaced rows.

Crops in pots

Containers are an obvious way to make the best use of space; and can instantly imbue your plot with its own style. Sleek metal, rustic terracotta, or quirky reclaimed containers, such as old sinks, and tin buckets and baths, can all look great. However, plants will be just as happy in functional plastic pots or growing bags, as long as they have good drainage.

Fill your containers with good-quality compost, mixed with water-retaining granules to help prevent them drying out. Since containers make plants mobile, you can move smaller planters into the sun, away from the wind, and under cover during winter, when necessary.

(above) **Even a tiny patio** has room for a few container-grown crops. They look attractive and can be moved around as required.

(above left) **Make a vegetable plot** on a windowsill. Small plants such as herbs will love the sun.

(left) **Hanging baskets** don't encroach on your growing space and look wonderful crammed with trailing tomatoes or edible flowers.

Be realistic

Hopes are invariably high when sowing gets under way in spring but, sadly, disappointment sometimes follows. To keep your enthusiasm going for years to come, it is vital to be realistic about what you are likely to achieve in the space and time you have available. Don't make the mistake of initially clearing a huge plot if you have only limited time to spend on it. Nothing is more disheartening than watching the weeds regain the upper hand after you have recently spent hours digging them out. It is better to start out small and expand as knowledge and experience increase. Success will soon build confidence.

There is no escaping the fact that whichever methods you use to grow fruit and vegetables, time and effort invested at every stage of the process are what bring good returns. Think carefully about how much you can plant without giving yourself an impossible amount of work later on.

Crop care

Planting directly into the soil involves early preparation, but once young plants are well established they usually grow happily without much input, except periodic weeding, watering during dry spells, and routine checks for pests and diseases.

Getting plants started in containers is initially less effort than planting in beds, but then you will have to spend time watering them, possibly twice daily in a hot summer, for as long as you want them to crop.

Keep it simple

If you have never grown your own before, keep it simple. Start with crops that are easy to cultivate and almost guaranteed to harvest. Buy in plants, so not everything has to be raised from seed.

Radishes, salads, potatoes, and beans are all reliable crops, while courgettes and tomatoes fruit all summer, paying back your investment if you choose to buy in plants. Leave challenging melons, cauliflowers, and grapes until you're confident with other crops.

(top) **Cut-and-come-again** salad leaves will produce several crops from just one sowing. They can be grown all year round.

(above) **If you want freshly picked greens** in midwinter, then try growing kale, one of the most resilient of all brassicas.

(left) **Asparagus** needs time and plenty of room to grow. It has a short season, but an established bed will crop for many years.

What to grow

It seems obvious, but use your space to grow what you like to eat. Although it's tempting to try weird and wonderful crops seen in catalogues, or to plant a glut of the latest superfood, what you really want is everyday produce that tastes fabulous. Even in a large garden there won't be time or space for everything, and to grow something to eat every day, you need to consider a few points.

The most important thing to weigh up is the return that each crop will give for the amount of space it takes. Asparagus, for example, needs a large dedicated bed to produce a decent crop over a couple of months. On the other hand, a few rows of cut-and-come-again leaves can keep a family in salad all year round. Many winter crops, such as parsnips and sprouting broccoli, need to be in the ground for months before they are ready for harvesting; so you either need to be clever and squeeze fast-growing crops between them or limit their numbers in small spaces.

Locally grown

You should also take into account which crops grow well locally. If you are not sure, find out by visiting nearby gardens, talking to your neighbours, or asking the growers at your local farmers' market. Use your common sense, too, when it comes to selecting crops that will do well on your plot. If you live in an area where the summers are cool and wet, then heat-loving crops such as aubergines and tomatoes will crop well only in a greenhouse or indoors. Gardeners in hot, dry climates may struggle to keep leafy salads and brassicas going during the height of summer.

It makes sense to put your effort into growing things that are either expensive or impossible to buy in the shops. What these crops might be depends on your local suppliers, but soft fruits, such as currants and berries are often pricey, as are herbs, runner beans, and good salad varieties. Globe artichokes, borlotti beans, and the full range of winter squashes are often simply unavailable, so if they take your fancy, why not grow your own?

If you have never harvested food fresh from the garden before then you might not know how incredibly different it can taste,

even compared to produce bought straight from the farmers' market. When there are just minutes between picking and eating, none of the precious sugars have been turned to starch and the cells are still plumped with water, so you get sweetness and crispness that simply cannot be bought. Some crops, including peas, beans, sweet corn, tomatoes, and new potatoes, lose this freshness faster than others, making them worth growing just because their flavour can't be matched in the shops.

(right) **Raspberries** often produce heavy crops that give you enough fruit to freeze or make into preserves, as well as to enjoy straight from the bush.

(below) **Freshly lifted new potatoes** have an incomparable flavour. You could grow a small crop in containers if you don't have room for a vegetable plot.

Smaller plots

Where space is at a premium, grow high-yielding fruit and vegetables that get the most out of every scrap of soil by cropping quickly or consistently over a long period. Look out for dwarf and bush varieties, bred to take up less room and often to grow well in containers. Use pots and grow bags and fill them with attractive varieties for a colourful display.

- **Bush tomatoes** – Great in hanging baskets, these can produce sweet cherry fruit for most of the summer.

- **Dwarf beans** – French and runner beans are available as dwarf varieties that crop heavily in a tiny space.

- **Herbs** – Both perennials and annuals deserve space for their long picking seasons and good looks.

- **Salad leaves** – Cut-and-come-again salads, like rocket and mizuna, will regrow three times in summer.

- **Blueberries** – These compact bushes thrive in pots; their berries ripen gradually for picking right through late summer.

- **Strawberries** – They look pretty in pots or at the edge of a border. Plant early, mid- and late varieties to extend the cropping period.

- **Summer radishes** – Ready to eat 6 weeks after sowing, peppery radish is perfect for filling a gap in your crops.

- **Beetroot** – The striking red-veined leaves look beautiful and are as good to eat as the earthy baby roots.

- **Swiss chard** – Neon-coloured stems make this leafy crop a must.

- **Courgettes** – A single bush can provide more than 20 fruits, along with glorious yellow flowers.

Growing under cover

This isn't some kind of covert gardening, but the practice of protecting plants from the worst weather, to extend the growing season. It is particularly useful if you live in a cold area where spring comes late and autumn early, but almost all gardeners looking to produce crops year-round will need to grow under cover at some stage.

(above) **Greenhouses** come in a range of materials and styles to suit all plots. They can be expensive, so consider buying a second-hand one locally.

(left) **Ideal growing conditions** are the main advantage of greenhouses and polytunnels, and they also provide somewhere to work in bad weather.

Grow indoors

Greenhouses and polytunnels take the lottery out of growing tender summer crops, providing the ideal environment to grow tomatoes, peppers, and aubergines, but you needn't stop there. Even unheated, these structures provide enough protection to grow extra early strawberries in spring, to raise winter crops such as radish and cut-and-come-again salads, and give many crops a head start.

Greenhouses are expensive to buy new, so make sure the shape and size you choose suits your garden and growing ambitions. Also ensure that there is adequate ventilation to keep air flowing around your plants; aim for one roof- and one side-vent for every 2m (6ft) of length.

Polytunnels are cheaper, but their functional appearance best suits allotments rather than gardens. The plastic that covers them has a limited lifespan, as does the plastic used in some greenhouses, and they are more difficult to ventilate, but they still provide a great growing space.

Whichever structure you choose, position it on a bright, level site, away from the shade of buildings and trees, and sheltered from strong winds. Be sure to provide good access, and try to find space outside for a rain barrel and also a tool shed.

Simple cover

Small-scale covers, such as cloches and cold frames, are invaluable for warming the soil to allow seeds to be sown early. They can also be used to harden off plants raised indoors, keep out damaging winds and hungry pests, and to protect overwintering crops.

Cloches, whether made of glass, plastic or fleece, are relatively cheap and have the advantage that they can be moved where needed, although they must be securely pinned to the soil. Use cut-off plastic bottles to cover individual plants, or low, wire-framed tunnels to protect whole rows.

Cold frames usually have a soil base and a sloping, glazed lid. Although lighter frames can be moved where required, most are permanently positioned against south-facing walls, to give maximum light and heat, and extra frost protection. They are ideal for raising early-sown seeds, hardening off young plants, or growing heat-loving crops like cucumbers and melons.

Plastic mini-greenhouses perform many of the same functions as a cold frame. Taller models are ideal for protecting growing bags planted with tomatoes, although they must be anchored securely, and have a sheltered, sunny site.

Even sunny windowsills are perfect for raising tender plants from seed. To stop seedlings bending towards the light, grow them in a simple light box made by cutting the front away from a small cardboard box, and lining the back with reflective silver foil.

(far left) **Cloches** provide enough warmth and protection to give crops a useful head start.

(left) **Mini-greenhouses** are ideal for tender crops, like tomatoes, if you have limited space. They can be easily packed away when not in use.

(below) **Cold frames** can be made from recycled materials to a size and shape to suit your plot. They can be permanent or temporary.

Contents

How to use this bookazine

This month-by-month guide takes you through all the stages of growing, tending and picking your own fruit and vegetables. Each chapter has an in-depth timeline, telling you what should be on your to do list for sowing, planting, harvesting and for all the other odd jobs around the garden or the allotment.

What to sow/plant
These pages offer clear advice on what to sow and plant, taking into account weather and climate. The central bar shows the final produce.

What to do
Use these pages as a calendar of tasks that will keep your crops and your growing space healthy. The central bar illustrates the development of that month's crops.

What to harvest
Pick your crops when they are at their best, especially, if you plan to store them. These pages help you identify when they are ripe and explain the best techniques for harvesting.

Gardening features
Each feature explains some of the best growing practices and techniques. They are relevant to the jobs for each month.

January: what to sow

EARLY-SEASON LEEKS

Early varieties of leek, such as 'King Richard' and 'Jolant', are best sown in January. They need a soil temperature of at least 8°C (46°F) in order to germinate, so a heated propagator in a greenhouse, or a cool room indoors, is essential for success. Sow seed thinly, about 1cm (½in) deep, into trays or modules filled with compost. Grow them on indoors, and the young plants will be ready to harden off and plant out later in spring.

HARVEST: **SEPT–APR**

TASTY SUMMER ONIONS

Maincrop onions need an early start, especially in colder areas where spring growth can be slow. Sow them indoors this month in a heated propagator at a temperature between about 10–15°C (50–59°F) and get them off to a flying start. Sow thinly, 1cm (½in) deep in trays and prick them out as they grow. Alternatively, sow about five seeds to a module and grow them on as little space-saving clusters of mature bulbs.

HARVEST: **JUL–OCT**

SOW

LEEKS

ONIONS

BROAD BEANS

LETTUCE

BROAD APPEAL

For early crops of broad beans, sow seed 5cm (2in) deep in modules or small pots, this month. Keep them under cover in a greenhouse or cold frame and they will be ready to plant out in early spring. Sow your beans outside only in a mild winter, with a temperature of at least 5°C (41°F), and give them some protection, such as garden fleece.

HARVEST: **MAY–AUG**

LETTUCE BEGIN

In mild areas, lettuces sown now under frames or cloches can be planted out in early spring for a really early supply of sweet salad. Sow thinly, 1cm (½in) deep, either in modules or in drills, 10cm (4in) apart. Look for early cos, butterhead, and loose-leaf salad-bowl varieties.

HARVEST: **APR–OCT**

CUT AND COME AGAIN

If you crave some fresh baby salad leaves, then try sowing a variety of cut-and-come-again crops under cover, either in the greenhouse or cold frame in beds, or in compost-filled boxes or seed trays. The best to try at this time of year are cress, salad rocket, sugar loaf chicory, or winter mixes, such as 'Oriental Saladini'. Scatter the seeds thinly, 1cm (½in) apart and cover with about ½cm (¼in) of soil before watering well. The leaves will be ready to harvest in a matter of 5–6 weeks.

● HARVEST: **ALL YEAR**

SALAD RADISH

Sow small-leaved radish, such as 'Saxa', in your unheated greenhouse borders or in large containers this month. Slow-growing, these varieties crop in winter, although may need extra protection with fleece or cloches on cold nights. Sow thinly, 1cm (½in) deep, in drills, 10cm (4in) apart. Thin the seedlings to 2cm (¾in) apart.

● HARVEST: **APR–NOV**

SALADS

RADISHES

PEAS

EARLY PEAS – THE EASY WAY

HARVEST: **JUN–OCT**

Peas, which you can sow indoors this month, hate root disturbance, so sow them in deep modules or a length of guttering to make transplanting easier.

1 PREPARE THE GUTTER
Cut plastic guttering into lengths that match the peas' final planting space. Block both ends, then fill them with seed compost.

2 SOW THE SEED
Choose dwarf early varieties and sow the seed 2cm (¾in) deep, 5cm (2in) apart. Standard gutter will accommodate two rows.

3 PLANT WHEN READY
When the seedlings are ready and hardened off, dig a gutter-sized trench and gently ease the entire length of compost into position.

January: what to do

STOCK UP

When bad weather keeps you indoors, spend some time comparing the catalogues of mail order seed suppliers. These offer a huge range of varieties to choose from, and you can shop around for competitive prices. Also take the opportunity to stock up on spring essentials such as pots, compost, seed trays, labels, stakes, and twine.

SOIL MAKEOVER

Double digging and incorporating manure is the best way to improve your soil before planting. It can be done in autumn or now, providing the soil isn't frozen.

1 DIG TRENCH ONE
Mark out the area being dug, dig out a trench two spades deep, and put the soil to one side.

2 DIG TRENCH TWO
Dig a second trench next to the first, turning the upper layer of soil into the base of the first trench.

3 ADD MANURE AND MIX
Add manure to the part-filled first trench, then the rest of the soil from trench two. Repeat.

TEND

GARDEN ESSENTIALS

FORCED FRUIT

BRASSICAS

DOUBLE DIGGING

EARLY WARMING

To encourage some of your plants, such as strawberries, to crop earlier than normal, in May instead of June, cover them now with cloches. The extra heat will allow them to flower and fruit earlier. This is also the time to place a rhubarb forcer over your plants to promote earlier stems that are sweeter and more tender. Remove the forcer in March and allow the plants to recover. Only force established plants.

STAY TIDY

As winter progresses, most hardy brassicas, including winter cabbages, sprouting broccoli, cauliflowers, and kales, tend to drop their more mature lower leaves. These can accumulate around the base, harbouring pests and diseases, and also start to smell. Pick up and compost fallen leaves regularly.

BAD APPLES
One bad apple can spoil all the rest, so check through your stored fruit for signs of brown rot fungus, damage from mice and other pests, or problems caused by fluctuating temperatures. Discard any diseased or spoiled produce, even if the damage is minimal. Make sure your store is well ventilated and insulated.

NEW FRUIT TREES
Most tree and bush fruits planted in late autumn need pruning as soon as they are in the ground. Cut blackcurrants right back so that all shoots have one bud above soil level. Redcurrant and gooseberry stems should be cut back by half, and raspberry and blackberry canes cut to 30cm (12in). On young, feathered maiden apple and pear trees, cut back the leading shoot and select lateral shoots to form the first branches. Don't prune cherries, plums, peaches, and apricots until spring.

FRUIT STORES

FRUIT PRUNING

WINTER PRUNING

PRUNE FRUIT TREES
Free-standing mature apple and pear trees need some winter pruning now to keep them fruiting well and to maintain an open, balanced shape. Your aim should be to remove any weak, congested, or damaged branches that are likely to be unproductive.

1 PRUNE TO SIDE BRANCH
To prune back to a side branch, undercut with a saw to about halfway through the stem. Make the final cut from above, to meet the undercut.

2 SHORTEN THIN BRANCHES
To encourage the formation of flowers in spring, cut back long spindly growth to a short branch, using sharp secateurs.

3 REMOVE WEAK GROWTH
If you have pruned your tree in previous years, check the old pruning sites and remove any weak stems growing round the cut areas.

4 PREVENT CONGESTION
Take out branches that are crossing over others, or growing towards the centre of the tree. This prevents congestion and disease.

January: what to harvest

TENDER BUDS

Early varieties of sprouting broccoli, such as 'Rudolph', sown last May, should start sending forth tender stems, topped with tight purple or white buds, this month. Be sure to cut or snap off shoots before they get too long and the flowers open, and each plant could keep cropping for up to 8 weeks. Sprouting broccoli is delicious lightly steamed or stir-fried, and has a sweet flavour. The shoots must be cut before the flowers open, so freeze any that you can't eat within 2–3 days, as they soon go past their best.

GRATE RADISH

Try to bite into one of these large hardy radishes in the same way that you would a summer salad variety, and you may be disappointed with their rather tough texture. Instead, these unusual vegetables are a treat when grated into salads, or cooked in hearty winter stews. Sown in July, they keep their flavour best when left in the ground, but if the weather turns bad, lift and store them in sand, like carrots.

HARVEST

CELERIAC

SPROUTING BROCCOLI

APPLES

WINTER RADISH

TWO CROPS IN ONE

This gnarled root vegetable, first sown in February, will survive in the soil through most winters, and can be pulled when required. Usefully, you can also cook and eat the leaves, which have a potent celery flavour. Try them added to soups or mixed with cabbage. To protect the roots in cold regions with regular hard frosts, cover the roots with fleece or a layer of straw.

IN STORE NOW

Not all apples will keep past Christmas, but in ideal storage conditions some dessert varieties, such as 'Pixie', and late culinary varieties, like 'Bramley's Seedling' and 'Howgate Wonder', will still be good to eat. Don't forget the sliced and stewed supplies squirrelled away in the freezer.

COUNT YOUR CHICONS

About 3–4 weeks after being plunged into darkness tasty, pale chicons, the forced new shoots of Witloof chicory, should be ready to harvest. Cut them about 2.5cm (1in) above the root with a sharp knife and eat the crisp, slightly bitter leaves raw in salads or braised. Chicons will keep in the fridge, but wrap them to exclude light and prevent them turning green. The cut root may re-sprout, giving a second crop, so don't forget to put it back in the dark. If it doesn't, discard the old root and start again.

SPRING GREENS

Cut-and-come salads can be sown throughout the year, and will crop through winter under cover, especially if you grow hardier varieties, such as corn salad. Pick regularly but sparingly, and try to alternate the plants you pick from, so they have time to re-grow. Only harvest healthy growth and discard any leaves damaged by frost.

WITLOOF CHICORY

CUT-AND-COME-AGAIN SALAD

GARLIC

CHECK YOUR STORED GARLIC

Planted in autumn or early spring and lifted the following summer, stored garlic bulbs start to sprout as spring approaches. Check your bulbs and roast them before they show green shoots.

SIGNS OF GROWTH
Discard any soft bulbs. Once one bulb shows signs of green shoots, the rest will quickly follow. Roast the bulbs to store for longer.

ROAST WHOLE
Remove any green shoots, drizzle olive oil over the bulbs and roast them in the oven at 180°C (350°F/ Gas 4) for about 30 minutes.

BACK IN STORAGE
Allow the garlic to cool before you store in jars under olive oil. Use the sweet-tasting cloves to flavour soups and stews.

DON'T FORGET

Keep a close eye on your stored crops, especially if they're still outside or in the garage or shed. Mice, birds, and many insects will be active in warmer spells, looking for something to eat.

Preparing a seedbed

Plants are at their most vulnerable as seeds and tiny seedlings. At this stage they need as near-perfect conditions as possible in which to germinate and grow quickly. Providing your seedlings with well-drained, weed-free soil that has been worked to a fine texture, will get them off to a good start. Time and effort spent on your seedbeds now will be well rewarded later with strong, healthy young plants.

Creating a tilth

Although seedlings do not need the most fertile soil, they are unlikely to thrive unless their environment has been prepared carefully beforehand. Creating what gardeners call a "fine tilth", where the soil surface is raked into fine crumbs, is important for successful germination, but this is easier on some soils than others. All soil types will benefit from the addition of a good organic compost. On heavy clay soils, working in a layer of sand helps to reduce stickiness and improve structure and drainage.

1 CLEAR WEEDS
Thoroughly weed the seedbed, taking care to remove whole perennial roots, like those of dandelions, which will regrow if left in the soil. Remove any large stones, too.

2 IMPROVE THE SOIL
Add a layer of well-rotted compost, as well as sand, to help drainage if you are working heavy clay. Dig the soil over lightly with a fork to break up the surface and work in the compost.

Jo's tips

If you want to create a nursery seedbed in which to raise young plants, such as brassicas, for transplanting, then choose a good open site rather than a neglected corner at the back of the garden.

Seedlings require sunshine, plenty of rain, and a soil that holds some moisture. Keep them away from the shade, shelter, and competing roots of tall trees and hedges as much as possible.

3 RAKE TO A TILTH
Firm the soil gently with the back of your rake, then move the rake backwards and forwards across the bed, removing stones, until you have a good, even, crumbly tilth.

4 MARK OUT A DRILL
Once you are happy with the soil texture, you can start sowing. Draw the pointed edge of a hoe through the soil to make a tidy drill at the correct depth for your chosen seeds.

Making a raised bed

Raised beds offer a low-maintenance way to grow your own crops, and suit busy lives and small spaces. They can be made from a range of materials, to heights and sizes to suit any plot. Because the beds can be constructed where there is no soil, or where the soil is poor, any bright spot can become a miniature allotment. They can provide temporary growing spaces, and be dismantled easily if you need the space.

Benefits

Raised beds make life easier: the paths between them mean you only have to dig, weed, and cultivate the area used for growing, and they can be filled with quality bought-in soil or compost, which reduces how much routine soil preparation you need to do. Where drainage is a problem they help lift plants clear of cold, wet earth. They also allow the soil to warm up more quickly in spring so that seeds can be sown sooner, giving your crops a useful head start.

Easy access

Avoid having to stand on your raised bed, compacting the soil with your feet, by making sure they are not too wide. Unless you are very tall, build your beds no more than 1.2m (4ft) across, so you can reach to the centre without over-stretching. Of course, beds can be narrower if you choose, and they can be whatever length and height you like. Taller beds are ideal for those who need plants in easy reach.

To provide a sound footing to work from when tending your bed, leave a wide path all the way around, preferably covered with weed-suppressing mulch.

OLD RAILWAY SLEEPERS
Lengthy sleepers make an excellent material for raised beds because you can build them up layer by layer to suit your needs. They are very heavy, so get help when moving them.

BRICKS
You can make beds any size and shape using bricks. They are also durable and maintenance-free. Brick beds must have drainage channels to prevent waterlogging.

RECYCLED MATERIALS
Many different materials can be used for beds, including wooden pallets, old water tanks, or even old tyres. Whatever you use, make sure it can support the weight of the soil safely.

February: what to sow

CRUNCHY CELERY
Celery and celeriac need a long growing season, so should be sown indoors at 10–15°C (50–59°F). Sow celeriac, 1cm (½in) deep in modules or seed trays, to crop autumn to spring. Sow celery on the surface of damp compost, to enjoy from summer to winter. Grow both on indoors, to harden off and plant out later in spring.

HARVEST: **VARIOUS**

CHILLI START
These heat-loving plants need a long, hot season to ripen well, and benefit from being sown early. Sow the seed indoors, 1cm (½in) deep, into pots or trays standing in a heated propagator, or on a warm windowsill. Keep them moist and warm, at around 21°C (70°F).

HARVEST: **JUL–OCT**

SOW

CELERY & CELERIAC

CHILLIES

BROAD BEANS & PEAS

GLOBE ARTICHOKES

SOW PEAS AND BEANS
If your soil isn't frozen or sodden, sow early broad bean outdoors, such as 'Super Aquadulce', to pick in May, plus early peas, like 'Feltham First', for a June crop.

HARVEST: **VARIOUS**

1 SOWING BEANS
Sow broad beans in drills, 25cm (10in) apart, using a dibber to bury them 5cm (2in) deep, and at 20–25cm (8–10in) intervals.

2 SOWING PEAS
Peas prefer warm soil and germinate better if cloched. Sow 4cm (1½in) deep, 8–10cm (3–4in) apart, in 20cm (8in) wide drills.

3 STILL TOO COLD?
If outdoor conditions aren't suitable for sowing, start beans off in modules, and sow peas in guttering under cover.

GOURMET VEG
Globe artichokes are gourmet vegetables that are expensive to buy, so it makes sense to grow your own. If you have space, and want plenty of these statuesque plants, the most economical way is to grow them from seed. Sow them 1cm (½in) deep in modules or trays in a propagator, or on a windowsill. Seed-raised plants can be variable, so only grow on the strongest seedlings.

HARVEST: **JUN–SEPT**

GROW BRASSICAS

Sow Brussels sprouts and kohl rabi 1cm (½in) deep in modules or trays in a heated propagator, or on a bright windowsill, to give them an early start. Choose early varieties of Brussels sprouts to sow now, for a tasty crop from winter to spring. Kohl rabi, sown in a propagator this month to crop in early summer, need planting out before the plants are 5cm (2in) tall to reduce the risk of bolting. This fast-growing vegetable can also be sown successively outdoors from early spring to late summer.

HARVEST: **VARIOUS**

SPEEDY SPINACH

Spinach is a fast-growing crop that can be prone to bolting when sown early. To help prevent this, sow the seed under cloches or in cold frames this month and next, using special 'short-day' varieties, such as 'Triathlon'. Sow the seed 1cm (½in) deep, in drills spaced about 30cm (12in) apart, thinning the seedlings 10–15cm (4–6in) apart.

HARVEST: **APR–NOV**

BRUSSELS & KOHL RABI

SPRING SPINACH

PARSNIPS

EARLY PARSNIPS

HARVEST: **NOV–APR**

If you live in a mild area, sow parsnips early for a long growing season, warming the soil with cloches or plastic to help improve germination.

1 MARKING OUT
Rake the seedbed to a fine tilth, removing any large stones. Make drills with a hoe, 2cm (¾in) deep and 30cm (12in) apart.

2 SPACE THE SEED
Sow three seeds per station, spaced 10cm (4in) apart. Cover the seed and water well. Parsnips are slow to germinate.

3 GROW THEM ON
Cover early sowings with cloches for best results, and thin seedlings to one per station. Protect plants from carrot fly.

DON'T FORGET

If you live in a colder region, this may be your first opportunity to sow leeks, lettuce, onions, cut-and-come-again salad, radish, and peas.

Indoors, grow sprouting seeds.

February: what to plant

CHOOSE RHUBARB

HARVEST: **MAR–JUL**

Although rhubarb is best planted in autumn, when newly dormant, you can also plant now when the new stems are about to sprout.

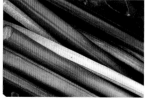

'CHAMPAGNE'
This variety produces long, vibrant red stems with a sharp, sweet taste. It is good for cooking.

'TIMPERLEY EARLY'
Is an early variety, ideal for forcing in spring, that giving a heavy crop of long, thick, juicy stems.

'VICTORIA'
A late variety, suitable for colder areas where early growth could be damaged by spring frost.

PLANT

JERUSALEM ARTICHOKES

SPRING GARLIC

RHUBARB

TASTY ARTICHOKES

Before planting these knobbly tubers, bear in mind that they grow up to 3m (10ft) tall. The plant tolerates all but the worst soil and some shade, and can be planted in under-used corners. Artichokes also make a good screen because of their height. Plant the tubers 10cm (4in) deep, about 30cm (12in) apart, and leave 90cm (36in) between rows for maximum harvests. These plants can be invasive.

HARVEST: **NOV–MAR**

LATE GARLIC

If you have heavy soil and find that over-wintered garlic rots in the ground, plant a spring variety such as 'White Solent'. Split the cloves and push them into the soil, flat end down, tops covered. Cloves planted in autumn under cover should be planted out now. Position 10cm (4in) apart, in rows with 25cm (10in) between them.

HARVEST: **JUL–AUG**

SHALLOTS AND LOTS OF ONIONS

Sets are small bulbs to plant now for an earlier crop than from seed-raised plants. Plant into well-prepared soil 2cm (¾in) deep.

HARVEST: **JUL–OCT**

Space onions 10cm (4in) apart, shallots 15cm (6in) apart, in rows spaced 30cm (12in). Delay planting onion sets if the weather is cold.

'RED BARON'
A productive onion with firm, dark red bulbs. Like all red varieties, it is mild enough to be eaten raw.

'STURON'
This is a maincrop onion, producing large, fleshy, brown-skinned bulbs. It has good resistance to bolting.

'LONGOR'
Described as a 'banana' shallot due to its elongated shape, this variety is easy to chop when cooking.

'RED SUN'
This is a red shallot, with white flesh and a mild flavour that can be eaten raw. It is good for pickling.

SHRUBBY HERBS

FRUIT TREES

ONIONS & SHALLOTS

HERBS IN POTS

HARVEST: **ALL YEAR**

Plant shrubby and evergreen herbs, such as bay, sage, and thyme in pots now to establish before summer.

1 PICK A POT
Choose a large enough container for the plant, make sure it has plenty of drainage holes, and part-fill it with soil-based compost.

2 POSITION THE PLANT
Position the plant at the same depth as in its own pot, 5cm (2in) below the rim of the container. Fill with more compost and water well.

FRUIT TREES

This is a good time to plant bare-root fruit bushes and trees while they are still dormant. Before planting, improve the soil, digging in well-rotted manure or compost. Dig a hole deep and wide enough so the roots can be spread out fully. Drive in a stake for trees. Plant to the same level as the soil line on the stem. Backfill the hole, firm in well, and water thoroughly.

HARVEST: **VARIOUS**

February: what to do

PROTECT BLOSSOM
Apricot and peach blossom opens so early in spring that it's highly vulnerable to damage from even relatively minor frosts. Damaged flowers will not set fruit. To protect your crop, cover the flowers with horticultural fleece draped over the branches. Protect wall-trained trees with a covered frame. Remove the fleece on warmer days to allow insects in for pollination – see below.

WALL-TRAINED FIGS
In cool regions, fig trees crop once a year, forming embryonic fruit near the tips of their summer shoots. These are carried through winter to ripen the following summer. Prune trees now to encourage new fruit-bearing growth on fan-trained trees in spring, cutting back half the shoots that carried fruit last summer to one bud. Tie the unpruned fruit-bearing shoots to the horizontal wires, filling in spaces in the framework.

TEND

FRUIT CANES

APRICOTS

PEACHES

FIGS

PRUNE CANE FRUIT
Autumn raspberries will fruit on canes produced this year, so cut all the canes back to the base now, before new growth appears. Summer raspberries and blackberries crop on last year's canes; these can be battered by harsh winter weather. Check your plants and cut any damaged tips back to a healthy bud. Secure any loose canes to their supports.

BE A BEE
Peaches and apricots come into flower this month, and must be pollinated if they're to produce fruit later in the year. If the weather remains cold, there will be few insects around to do the job. To ensure a crop, use a small, soft paintbrush to transfer pollen between flowers. Don't forget any trees covered against frost.

WINTER PRUNING

This is the last chance to prune your currant and gooseberry bushes while they are still dormant. Prune up to a third of the older shoots at the base from your blackcurrant bushes. Also trim back by half the leading shoots of gooseberries; red- and whitecurrants, cut back sideshoots to two buds, and remove any dead or overcrowded wood to open up the centre of the bush. You can also prune cobnuts now by shortening long sideshoots, which you may have "brutted" last summer, to three or four buds.

TURN COMPOST

This is a quiet month in the garden so take the opportunity to turn your compost heap. All heaps need to be turned at least once. Using a fork, break up any matted lumps, and move drier, uncomposted material from the top and edges of the heap, to the centre. If the contents are mostly composted, empty the heap now and start again.

FRUITS & NUTS

COMPOST

EARLY POTATOES

CHIT POTATOES

To give your early potatoes a head start and produce a better crop, start the tubers into growth indoors – chitting. This isn't necessary with maincrops.

1 CHECK TUBERS
To plant out in 6 weeks' time, check through your seed potatoes now and discard any that are shrivelled or diseased.

2 STAND IN BOXES
Take each tuber and find the end with the most buds or eyes. Stand it, this end up, in a box in a cool, light, frost-free place.

3 PLANT OUT
Stocky shoots should develop from each eye. When these are about 2.5cm (1in) long the tubers are ready for planting out.

DON'T FORGET

Take care when clearing fallen leaves and other debris, or turning the compost heap, as at this time of year they may be sheltering beneficial animals, such as frogs, toads, and hedgehogs.

February: what to harvest

HEEL IN PARSNIPS

These large roots take up a lot of space, which is needed now for new seedbeds. To make room for spring planting, lift your remaining parsnips and store them in another part of the garden. Using a fork, carefully ease out the parsnips, taking care not to damage the roots, and heel them in elsewhere. Heeling-in simply involves digging a shallow-angled trench, where the roots can be laid close together and covered with soil. They will take up far less space and can be unearthed as required.

LAST CHANCE FOR SWEDES

If you left part of your swede crop to overwinter in the ground, now is the time to dig up any remaining roots. Even if they survive for longer without rotting or pest damage, they will become increasingly woody and inedible. This is your last chance to make use of the crop, and a good moment to clear ground that will soon be needed for new plantings. It's also worthwhile checking swedes in storage for pest damage or decay.

HARVEST

PARSNIPS

SWEDES

WINTER SALAD

WINTER CUT-AND-COME-AGAIN

Winter salads needn't be dull. Many leafy crops can be grown under cover as cut-and-come-again salad at this time of year. Once the leaves are the size you prefer, cut them with scissors 2cm (¾in) above the soil and a new crop should regrow in a few weeks.

CHERVIL
This is commonly grown as a herb, and has a mild, parsley-like flavour. It can also be harvested as young leaves to spice up your salads.

TATSOI
This salad leaf has a mild, mustard flavour and a crisp texture, and can be eaten raw or cooked. The plants are very hardy, ideal for cold areas.

ROCKET
A few leaves of peppery tasting rocket can transform a salad. Cut the leaves when they are new and fresh, as they turn bitter when older.

PERPETUAL SPINACH
The tender new leaves are delicious either in salads or cooked. Cut them from alternate plants to leave room for new growth along the row.

INDOOR HERBS

It's a real treat to have fresh herbs to pick throughout winter. Container-grown herbs, such as marjoram, mint, thyme, and parsley, will continue to thrive on the windowsill or in the conservatory with minimal attention. As long as you ensure that the plants are warm and watered, they should keep new growth coming until it's time for them to go back outdoors in spring. Use scissors to snip off the fresh tips when required.

LIFT ARTICHOKES

Jerusalem artichokes don't store well, so it's best to dig them up as required. Unearth the tubers with a fork, being careful not to spear any. Remove even unusably small ones, because they will regrow in spring if left in the soil. Scrub the tubers with a brush, peel them, and use quickly for soups and side dishes before they discolour.

HERBS

JERUSALEM ARTICHOKES

LEEKS

ENDIVE

LATE LEEKS

Late-season leek varieties are very hardy and will stand in the ground until spring without spoiling their texture or flavour. Lift them as required with a fork. Their roots can hold on tightly, so loosen the soil to a good depth, to allow the leek to pull away without breaking. To avoid carrying a lot of soil into the kitchen, cut off the roots and drop them on the compost heap.

CUT ENDIVE

Endives growing under cover should resprout after cutting, so never uproot a plant when harvesting. Instead, cut the base of a mature endive head with a sharp knife and trim off any damaged leaves. Endives will keep for several days somewhere cool, as long as they are not stored damp.

Sowing under cover

Even if you are new to vegetable growing, you will probably want to sow some crops under cover, and the advantages are undeniable. Sowing early, and providing additional warmth and shelter, gives tender plants a useful head start, allowing them to crop sooner and for longer. Seedlings raised under cover also often show stronger growth than those sown directly outside – and give better harvests.

A protected environment

There is nothing complicated about sowing seeds under cover, and it is not necessary to have a greenhouse. You simply need to give your plants a protected environment, whether you sow them in trays, or individual pots, or modules. The protection you provide could consist of a cold frame, a cloche, or just a sunny windowsill indoors.

Seedling plants under cover can be highly susceptible to diseases. You should constantly monitor their conditions to ensure that warmth and humidity are maintained at the correct levels.

1 PREPARE SEED TRAYS
Fill seed trays to about 1cm (½in) from the top with a good multipurpose compost. Firm lightly, using the base of another tray or your fingers. Water well and allow to drain.

2 SOW SEEDS
Sow small seeds thinly over the surface, shaking them carefully from the packet or your hand. Plant larger seeds deeper, using a dibber or pencil to make a hole for each seed.

3 ADD TOP LAYER
Use a sieve to distribute a fine layer of compost over the seeds. Larger seeds may need soil pushed over them with a dibber. If your seeds are very small, try not to disturb them.

4 WATER GENTLY
Damp down the compost, using a watering can with a fine rose and taking care not to overwater. You should maintain this level of watering throughout germination.

5 COVER THE TRAY
To create a warm, moist atmosphere for germination, place the seed tray in a heated propagator. Alternatively, you can cover the tray with a plastic lid or sheet of glass.

Pricking out seedlings

As soon as your seeds have germinated, turn down the heat in the propagator or remove the lid from the tray, to help prevent fungal diseases. When the seedlings are large enough to handle, prick them out to grow on in individual pots.

6 LIFT SEEDLINGS
Holding each seedling very lightly by either of its first leaves, use a dibber or pencil to ease the plant out of the compost. Take care not to pull on the fragile roots.

7 PLANT INDIVIDUALLY
Fill individual pots or multi-celled seed trays with new compost and transfer the seedlings one at a time. Grow them on until they are sturdy enough to be planted out.

Sowing outside

Sowing directly into the soil is the simplest and cheapest way to raise vegetables. Preparing your seedbed well, sowing at the right depth, and getting the timing right can make the difference between a lush row of healthy plants and a frustratingly patchy harvest.

Good preparations

It is much easier to distinguish germinating vegetables from weed seedlings if they come up in a straight line. To achieve this, mark out your row by running string between pegs pushed into the ground at either end.

Sow larger seeds deeper than smaller ones. As a rule, make your drill three times as deep as the seed. When you have sown your seeds (as illustrated below), carefully pull the soil across the drill to cover them, using a hoe or rake, or your hands.

Label the row clearly before removing the string line, because it is all too easy to forget what you have sown and where. Water the seeds in thoroughly, using a can fitted with a fine rose to avoid washing them away.

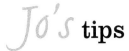

Jo's tips

Never sow into cold, wet soil as seeds may rot, or if they do come up, they're likely to bolt. Delay sowing until the weather improves or cloche the soil to warm it. Always protect seedbeds from mice, birds, or cats.

1 SOWING IN A DRILL
To make a drill, run the point of a hoe, or a bamboo cane, along the string line at a consistent depth. Pour seeds into the palm of your hand, take a pinch and sprinkle them thinly.

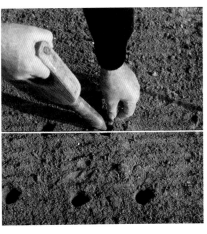

2 STATION-SOWING
To reduce the need for thinning out, try 'station-sowing'. Mark the row and use a dibber to create stations at the right depth and spacings for your crop. Sow three seeds in each station.

SOWING INSIDE AND OUTSIDE

March: what to sow

TWO ROOTS
To prevent them bolting, sow summer beetroot and turnips in soil warmed under cold frames or cloches or in a greenhouse. Try bolt-resistant 'Boltardy' beetroot or turnip 'Purple Top Milan'. In drills 20cm (8in) apart, sow seed 1cm (½in) deep. Thin beetroot to 8cm (3in) apart, and leave 10cm (4in) between turnips.

HARVEST: **VARIOUS**

EASY CALABRESE
Unlike other brassica crops, calabrese does not transplant well from seedbeds. So, either sow directly outside at its final spacing of 30cm (12in) each way, or sow into modules outdoors or in a cold frame. You can then plant the seedlings out at the same spacing.

HARVEST: **JUN–OCT**

SOW

BRASSICAS

BEETROOT & TURNIPS

SPRING ONIONS

CALABRESE

BRASSICA BASICS
Sow summer cabbage and cauliflowers now to crop in summer and autumn. Sprouting broccoli sown this month will produce spears in winter and early spring. To make more of your space, sow them in 1cm (½in) deep drills in a seedbed, and transplant to their final spacing 5–6 weeks later. Net the young plants to keep pigeons off.

HARVEST: **VARIOUS**

NON-STOP ONIONS
For a constant supply of full-flavoured salad onions throughout the year, start sowing outdoors now, and continue making further successional sowings every 2–3 weeks all summer. Weed the bed thoroughly first and make narrow drills about 10cm (4in) apart. Sow the seed very thinly, about one seed every 2cm (¾in), to reduce the need for thinning out later on.

HARVEST: **ALL YEAR**

AUBERGINES – BLACK MAGIC

HARVEST: **AUG–OCT**

Sow seeds 1cm (½in) deep, prick out, and pot them on once the seedlings reach 5cm (2in). Keep the seeds at a minimum temperature of 20°C (68°F).

'MONEYMAKER'
This is a reliable, early variety, that produces large, deep purple fruit. Suitable for growing indoors or out, and also in patio containers.

'CALLIOPE'
Almost free of spines, this compact variety produces an abundance of small, 10cm (4in) long fruit. Pick often to ensure a sustained crop.

'BLACK ENORMA'
As its name suggests, this variety produces exceptionally large pure black fruit. Just two or three plants should keep you going.

STILL TIME TO SOW

In warm areas, sow outside: broad beans, onion, leeks, peas, rocket, parsnips, and spinach. Inside sow: radish, lettuce, celeriac, celery, globe artichoke, Brussels, and kohl rabi.

TOMATOES, PEPPERS & CHILLIES

CARROTS

AUBERGINES

CROPS FOR SALSA

For indoor crops of tomatoes, peppers and chillies, sow now at about 20°C (68°F), in a heated propagator or on a warm windowsill. Sow about 2cm (¾in) deep in modules or seed trays, and make sure seedlings get plenty of light to stop them getting tall and leggy. Prompt pricking out and potting on will give plants plenty of space, and ensure strong specimens. For outdoor crops, only sow when frosts are less severe, so the plants won't be ready too early to plant out.

HARVEST: **JUL–OCT**

COSY CARROTS

Carrots won't germinate in cold soil, so sow them now under cloches, and remove them as the weather warms. Choose early varieties like 'Early Nantes' and 'Parmex'. Rake the seedbed to a fine tilth and sow thinly in drills 1cm (½in) deep, 15cm (6in) apart. Early crops usually miss the worst carrot fly attacks.

HARVEST: **MAY–DEC**

March: what to plant

A BUNCH OF CAULIFLOWERS

Early summer cauliflowers, sown in autumn and overwintered under cover are now ready for hardening off and planting out into their final positions. Choose good, firm soil, with a pH of 6.5–7.5, avoiding beds manured the previous autumn or those where brassicas have recently been grown. Plant each cauliflower about 50cm (20in) from the next, because they will develop into large plants. Place collars round the base of each to protect against cabbage root fly and net against pigeons, if necessary.

HARVEST: **JUN–AUG**

SPRING SPINACH

Spinach plants sown under cover last month should be planted out now, after hardening off, to be ready for cropping later in spring. Plants can reach a good size, so space them 15cm (6in) apart with a distance of 30cm (12in) between rows, and protect them again with cloches if conditions turn cold. The lushest growth is produced on plants growing in rich, moist soil in full sun, so site plants accordingly.

HARVEST: **APR–NOV**

PLANT

PEAS

CAULIFLOWERS

GRAPES

SPINACH

SUMMER PEAS

Harden off young peas, sown in January, and plant in fertile soil and full sun. Dig a shallow trench for those sown into guttering and slide the plants into it in one go, to reduce root disturbance. Module-raised peas should be planted 5–8cm (2–3in) apart. Insert supports, such as pea sticks, or canes and netting.

HARVEST: **JUN–OCT**

GROW GRAPES

On a sheltered site in full sun, fix horizontal support wires to a wall or to sturdy wooden posts – a south-facing wall is ideal. Improve the soil with compost. Plant vines 1.2m (4ft) apart and 25cm (10in) from the support base, and firm in well. Ensure the graft union scar is above soil level.

HARVEST: **OCT–NOV**

BUDDING BROAD BEANS

After a short period of hardening off, plant out broad bean seedlings, sown in February, 15cm (6in) apart with 23cm (9in) between rows in full sun and good rich soil. In sheltered spots dwarf varieties like 'The Sutton' may not need support, but if in doubt a simple system of stakes along each side of the row, with string or wire fastened between them will be enough to keep mature plants standing. Remember not to plant broad beans where they, or other peas or beans, have recently been grown.

HARVEST: **MAY–AUG**

PLANT BERRIES

Blackberries are tough plants and will tolerate slightly poor drainage, some shade, and even late frosts, but such hazards are best avoided. Improve the planting area with plenty of compost, and plant each cane to the depth it was in its pot, spaced 4m (12ft) apart. They require post and wire supports to keep the growth manageable.

HARVEST: **JUL–OCT**

BROAD BEANS

BLACKBERRIES

FIRST EARLY POTATOES

PLANT POTATOES

HARVEST: **JUN–SEP**

Plant first earlies if the ground isn't frozen. Their roots help to break up newly cultivated earth and they like a sunny site, with deep, fertile soil.

1 CHITTING
Chitted tubers give a quicker crop than unchitted. Dig 15cm (6in) deep drills, at least 38cm (15in) apart to give them plenty of room.

2 PLANTING
Carefully place a potato 'rose-end' up in the bottom of the drill every 30cm (12in), trying not to damage the shoots.

3 COVERING
Rake soil over to cover the row. If the weather is cold, a thick mulch of compost or well-rotted manure will help protect the tubers.

DON'T FORGET

Frosts may be less severe this month but keep cloches, fleece, and even sheets of newspaper handy to protect emerging crops on cold nights. Also protect young plants from slugs and snails.

March: what to do

CLEAR FOR CULTIVATION
Mulches help suppress weeds in beds where crops are growing or in areas being cleared for cultivation. Black landscaping fabric (see left) is permeable to rain, so is useful for growing crops through, but you might need to irrigate beneath it. You could also cover large weedy areas for a few months with old carpet to kill off perennial weeds before cultivation. Organic mulches, such as compost or straw, should be laid at least 5cm (2in) thick. As well as discouraging weeds, they add organic matter to the soil.

WAR ON WEEDS
Weeds compete with seedlings for light, moisture, and nutrients, so give your vegetables a head start by removing all weeds from seedbeds and planting areas. Annual weed seedlings can simply be hoed off and the debris raked up. Perennial weeds need to be dealt with more rigorously. Dig them out with a fork and make sure you remove every scrap of their roots. If you don't, most of them will regrow in a short time.

TEND

SUPPRESS WEEDS

DIG OUT WEEDS

HERBS

MULCH

HELP FOR HERBS
Encourage a fresh flush of fragrant leaves on perennial herbs such as rosemary, marjoram, sage, and thyme, by pruning them back before growth starts. This treatment also helps keep plants compact and an attractive shape. With perennials that die right back, such as mint and fennel, clear away any of last year's dead stems to make way for new shoots.

IMPROVE SOIL
To get the best from your fruit trees and bushes it's important to keep their soil in good heart, particularly if you garden on a light sandy soil. Lay a generous mulch of compost or well-rotted manure, at least 5cm (2in) thick, at the base of each plant, allowing space around the canes or trunk to avoid the risk of rot.

SPRING BOOST

Crops that have come through a hard winter can look distinctly the worse for wear at this time of year. If your cabbages, purple sprouting broccoli, kale, or overwintered onions have yellowing leaves, it's a sure sign that they could do with an early spring boost. To perk them up, apply a balanced fertilizer this month.

BEDS FOR BEANS

Climbing beans and celery grow best on a rich soil that retains plenty of moisture. To encourage strong growth, prepare their beds in advance of planting. A traditional way to provide the right conditions involves digging a trench about 30cm (12in) deep and 45cm (18in) wide. Work in plenty of well-rotted manure or household compost as you backfill the trench. Beans are legumes and supply their own nitrogen, so if manure and compost are scarce, use kitchen peelings to help retain moisture.

FEED

PREPARE THE SOIL

SEEDLINGS

PRICK OUT SEEDLINGS

If your propagator or windowsill is full of tomato, pepper, celery, or other seedlings, start pricking them out into individual pots.

1 REMOVE FROM TRAY
Using a small dibber or pencil, loosen the roots of each seedling and lift it from the compost by the first pair of leaves, not by its stem.

2 REPOT
Plant out in separate modules. Make a hole with the dibber and replant the seedling. Gently firm the compost and water in.

3 HARDEN OFF
To acclimatize the seedlings to outdoor conditions, harden them off in a cold frame with a lid that can be opened and closed.

DON'T FORGET

Pests are beginning to emerge this month, so look out for snail trails and signs of marauding insects. Decide how you want to approach pest control and be ready to take action.

March: what to harvest

TASTY FLORETS
After a May sowing and the winter spent outside, hardy cauliflowers, such as 'Winter Aalsmeer', should start developing their large, white curds this month. Cauliflowers are best cut while the curds are still firm and healthy, or else the heads can yellow and open. They do, however, have a tendency to all come at once. Split into florets and freeze surpluses or pickle them.

RED STALKS
In good weather, rhubarb will start sending up tasty red-tinted stems. Only harvest from mature plants over 2 years old, picking what you need by gripping them near the base and pulling. Don't cut the stems as the stump left can encourage rot to set into the crown.

HARVEST

WINTER CAULIFLOWER

RHUBARB

CHICORY

CABBAGE & SPROUTS

THE BITTER END
Bitter-leaved, red and sugarloaf chicory, sown in late summer and grown under cover through the winter, will be coming to an end this month. Red-types, such as 'Palla Rossa Verona', can either be harvested by cropping individual leaves, or cutting the whole head with a sharp knife just above ground level. Cut the heads whole of sugarloaf varieties, like 'Pan de Zucchero'. Even at this late stage both types may re-sprout to provide further harvests, so if their space isn't needed for another crop, leave them in the ground to grow on for now.

LAST BRASSICAS
New spring crops may be just around the corner, but don't be tempted to overlook the last of your hardy winter brassicas. Having started at the bottom, you'll probably be picking near the tops of the stems of late sprout varieties, such as 'Exodus' and 'Trafalgar', by now. When the sprouts are finished, remember to cut the delicious leafy tops, too. You should also pull up or cut winter cabbages as required, trimming away any weather-damaged outer leaves. After harvesting, dig up the roots. If there are any signs of disease, such as clubroot, burn them – don't compost them.

GROW BETTER BEET

Swiss chard and spinach beet sown in late summer survive most winters outdoors and come into growth again this month, with fresh leaves to crop. Cut back old battered growth and pull bright new leaves away at the base. The succulent stems are good to eat.

'RHUBARB CHARD'
As its name suggests, this variety has ruby-red stems and purple-flushed foliage, much like rhubarb. It is also good for winter colour.

'LUCULLUS'
This is a prolific chard that gives a good crop of white-stemmed leaves. Like all beet, its stems can be cooked and served like asparagus.

'BRIGHT YELLOW'
All beet comes into crop early in spring, providing tender new leaves. Use this variety raw to add a cheery splash of colour to your salads.

PERPETUAL SPINACH BEET
Easy to grow, this thin-stemmed variety is hardier than true spinach, and gives a reliable, tasty crop. It is a good choice for drier soil.

STORED ROOTS

SPRING ONIONS

LEAF BEETS

ROOT CHECK

Any lifted and stored winter root crops, like carrots and beetroot, will need using up in soups and stews as soon as possible. Check through them and discard any that are showing signs of decay. Don't be tempted to bring what's left indoors to keep in the fridge, because they will shrivel up and spoil much faster there than in their original stores.

EARLY ONIONS

Start harvesting hardy varieties of spring onions, such as 'White Lisbon' and 'Ramrod', sown in late summer or early autumn, and overwintered outside. If the soil has become compacted around the bulbs, loosen it with a hand fork before picking – the onions can easily break if pulled too hard.

Growing mushrooms

Mushrooms are an unusual crop but once you've grasped the basic technique, they're easy to grow and can provide a worthwhile harvest from unused spots outdoors, or in a dark corner inside. The familiar white and brown cap mushrooms are the quickest and easiest, but you can also grow more exotic species, like oyster mushrooms.

1 **It's simple to grow** your own white cap mushrooms from a kit at any time of year, as long as you have the correct growing conditions. Pour the specialist compost into the tray or container provided. Break up lumps.

2 **Moisten the compost** thoroughly. Carefully open the packet of mushroom spawn and scatter it evenly over the compost. Gently mix it into the surface using your hand or a hand fork. Don't mix the spores in deeply.

3 **Cover the container** with the lid or use layers of damp newspaper. Place it somewhere at around 15°C (59°F) and keep it moist. Mushrooms don't need to be in the dark, just out of direct sunlight; a shed would suit.

4 **After about 14 days**, web-like mycelium should be visible on the surface. Remove any newspaper and cover the mycelium with 2.5cm (1in) of compost, keeping it moist. The first mushrooms will appear in 10 weeks.

TRY THESE

There are many different types of mushroom and growing kits to try at home. Some are more complicated than others – just follow the instructions given.

White cap mushrooms – Much tastier when home-grown, these are quick and easy to grow throughout the year.

Oyster mushrooms – Grown outdoors on logs, you'll need patience until these bear fruit in spring and autumn.

Shiitake mushrooms – These are grown on logs, shocked into fruiting by soaking in cold water for 48 hours.

Brown cap mushrooms – Also known as chestnut mushrooms, these are grown in the same way as white caps.

GROWING MUSHROOMS

April: what to sow

SOW ON CUE
Sow cucumbers, courgettes, and summer squash at the end of the month to give them a head start, especially those you plan to grow under cover. Sow them 2cm (¾in) deep in small pots and put in a heated propagator, or on a warm windowsill. Keep cucumbers at 20°C (68°F) and the courgettes and squash at 15°C (59°F).

HARVEST: **JUL–OCT**

BEAN FEAST
For an early start for French and runner beans, warm the soil with cloches and sow beneath them, or sow into modules or pots under cover, 5cm (2in) deep, and plant out later. If sowing outside, space climbing beans 30cm (12in) apart, and dwarf beans, 20cm (8in) apart.

HARVEST: **JUL–OCT**

SOW

CUCUMBER & COURGETTE

MELONS

FENNEL & ENDIVE

BEANS

TRY MELONS
HARVEST: **AUG–SEP**

Sow two seeds, 2cm (¾in) deep in small pots at 18°C (64°F). Once germinated, thin the weakest, water sparingly and grow the plants on a few degrees cooler.

'BLENHEIM ORANGE'
This is a traditional variety, with netted, green skin and orange-red flesh. It has a good flavour, and is suitable for cooler regions.

CANTALOUPE
This is a type of melon, not just a variety, and produces small fruit with yellow skins and flesh. Good in cooler areas, even outdoors.

'ANTALYA'
This is a galia-type melon, with netted, yellow skin and sweet, green flesh. Grow under cover as it prefers warmer conditions.

LUXURY VEG
Sow Florence fennel and endive to crop during the summer. Raise plants in modules under cover to transplant later, or sow seed directly outdoors if the soil is above 10°C (50°F) — Florence fennel may bolt in colder soil. Sow seed 1cm (½in) deep. Outdoors, sow thinly in drills 25cm (10in) apart for endive, 30cm (12in) apart for Florence fennel. Thin the seedlings promptly.

HARVEST: **VARIOUS**

GROW GREENS

Sow kale this month, such as 'Black Tuscan', to harvest in autumn and winter, plus summer and autumn cauliflowers. Sow them outdoors into drills or modules, 1cm (½in) deep, thinning those sown in the soil to 8–10cm (3–4in) apart. Grow the plants on and transplant them into their final positions in June. Space kale plants 45cm (18in) apart, and the cauliflowers 60cm (24in), and water well. Cover the seedlings and young plants with nets in areas where pigeons can be a problem.

HARVEST: VARIOUS

LETTUCE SEASON

You can sow lettuce seed almost all year but now is peak season. Sow seed thinly, 1cm (½in) deep, either directly in rows, 20–35cm (8–14in) apart, depending on variety, or in modules to plant out later. The latter method is ideal for plants to pop into odd gaps or pots. Be vigilant, because slugs will find young lettuce seedlings quickly.

HARVEST: MAY–NOV

ASPARAG

SWEET CORN

KALE & CAULIFLOWERS

SUMMER LETTUCE

PL...
Spri...
in f...

1

20cm
aspa...
high

SWEET CORN FOR SUMMER

HARVEST: AUG–OCT

Sweet corn prefers warm growing conditions, but if you live in a mild area, sow it outdoors under cloches once the soil temperature is above 13°C (55°F).

1 MARKING OUT
Sweet corn make tall plants, so give them space. Station sow seeds 35cm (14in) apart, in rows with 60cm (24in) between them.

2 BLOCK PLANTING
The flowers are pollinated by wind, which is essential for the cobs to form fully. Plant in blocks to help ensure good pollination.

3 SOWING INDOORS
If you live in a cooler area, sow seed singly, 4cm (1½in) deep, in modules or pots, under a cold frame or in a greenhouse.

STILL TIME TO SOW

Outside sow: leeks, onion, peas, parsnips, Brussels, kohl rabi, spinach, cabbage, turnips, and carrots.
Indoors: celeriac, calabrese, tomatoes, peppers, and aubergines.

April: what to harvest

FIRST SUMMER SPINACH

Start picking the first baby salad leaves now, from spinach plants sown under cover in early spring. Pick them regularly to encourage further crops, but leave some plants to develop unmolested, to give you a harvest of full-sized plants for cooking later in summer. Cooked spinach freezes well, but the baby leaves growing now are best eaten fresh. Give time to re-grow.

KALE HEARTS

The kale season is about to close but the plants will soon be producing fresh young leaves at their centres, which are far more appetizing than the winter-worn, outer ones. Crop these leaves, then uproot and compost the plants as they finish.

PLANT

HARVEST

RADISHES

SPINACH

ROCKET

KALE

RAPID RADISH

Hot and peppery, these feisty roots can be ready to eat just 3 weeks after sowing. They soon spoil quickly, so pull them as soon as they're ready.

'CHERRY BELLE'
This is a quick maturing variety that produces small, rounded radish that are sweet and mild. They are delicious whole in salads.

'FRENCH BREAKFAST'
This variety takes about a month to mature from sowing, and produces mild, crunchy roots that are just long enough to eat sliced.

'SCARLET GLOBE'
This is a quick-growing variety with bright red skin and crisp white flesh. It is ready to harvest after 6–8 weeks; sow successionally.

ROCKET SPEED

These delicious, peppery leaves are ready to pluck in as little as 3 weeks from sowing. Pick leaves individually or use scissors to cut entire rows of plants, 2.5cm (1in) above the soil surface. Feed and water to encourage new growth, then re-harvest at least once more. If you then let them run to seed, you can use the creamy flowers to decorate salads. The leaves and flowers are best eaten fresh.

SPRING GREENS

If you've plenty of spring cabbages, sown last July, harvest some now as spring greens before they heart-up, leaving others to develop. If you don't need the space for other crops, cut the cabbages above their lowest leaves, rather than uprooting the plant. The stalks often re-sprout to produce a second crop of small heads.

EARLY STRAWBERRIES

Early varieties of strawberries, brought under cover in January, should be coming into fruit by the end of this month. Wait until the fruit has turned completely red before picking it with the stalk intact. If you just have a few plants, the berries will be a treat to eat while you're out gardening. If you have a larger crop, they should still be eaten as soon after picking as possible to be at their best. Failing that, use them for early jam.

SHOOTS & LEAVES

SPRING CABBAGE

STRAWBERRIES

TASTY TIPS

With so much fresh growth around it's worth taking a tour of your vegetable and herb patch for pickings to perk up a plain salad. Most crops won't miss a few leaves and shoots, just pick sparingly so you don't check the later development of your mature crops.

SWISS CHARD

The baby leaves of Swiss chard add colour to the vegetable patch with their bright stems. They have a sweet, earthy flavour.

PEA SHOOTS

Peas benefit from being pinched out, which is handy as the shoots have a delicious sweet flavour. Just snip off the topmost leaves.

HERBS

The young leaves of many herbs often have the most intense flavour. Try picking the new shoots of basil, coriander, and marjoram.

BEETROOT

Beetroot gives two crops in one. Pick a few red-veined leaves for salads, and enjoy eating the earthy-tasting roots a couple of weeks later.

Patio fruit and vegetables

Don't be deterred if the only area you have for your kitchen garden is a paved patio or courtyard, because these are often designed to make the most of sunny, sheltered spots that are ideal for growing fruit and vegetables. Many crops thrive in containers, and although the harvests will be smaller, they're no less rewarding.

PLANTING IDEAS

Container cropping

Growing fruit and vegetables in containers has many advantages over gardening in open soil. For a start there's no heavy digging to do, and you can select the perfect compost for every plant. Weeding should be minimal and less back-breaking because the pots raise the soil surface; this makes picking crops easier too. Containers can also be moved to take advantage of summer sun or winter shelter, as required.

Herbs and salads are great for beginners, but tomatoes, chillies, aubergines, and even root crops in deep pots, should all thrive, especially dwarf and patio varieties. Even fruit trees and bushes will crop well in large containers, once established, so don't feel you have to miss out if you're gardening in a small space.

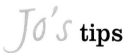

Jo's tips

Routine feeding and watering of fruit and vegetable plants in pots is vital if you want a good harvest. Water them generously once or twice a day during summer, and apply a balanced liquid feed to root and leaf crops, or a high potash feed to fruiting crops, weekly during the growing season.

ENSURE GOOD DRAINAGE
Before planting, check there are adequate holes in the bottom of the container. If not, carefully drill some or use another pot. Place broken polystyrene or shards of clay pot in the bottom to improve drainage.

USE THE RIGHT COMPOST
Single-season crops, such as lettuce, can be planted into potting compost. Trees, shrubs, and perennial crops such as rhubarb, are best planted into a longer-lasting, soil-based compost, such as John Innes No.3.

FOOD AND MOISTURE
To help prevent your crops drying out, and to keep them well fed, incorporate water-retaining gel crystals and slow-release granular fertilizer into the compost before planting.

CLIMBING CROPS IN POT
To grow climbing vegetables, such as peas and runner beans, insert canes into the compost to form a wigwam. Plant seedlings or direct sow seed at the base of each cane.

TRY THESE

Almost any large, durable container with good drainage is suitable for crops, so be creative. Try recycling old cans, tin baths, crates, and sacks.

Windowboxes are ideal for herbs and low-growing crops that you might want to pick from the kitchen window.

Growing bags are incredibly versatile, and can be used inside or out for a huge range of fruit and vegetables.

Recycled containers can be as varied as your crops. Try growing potatoes in old bins and leeks in builder's bags.

Clay and concrete pots look good on the patio, although they can be heavy and prone to frost damage.

Summer fruit growing in containers can be attractive as well as productive. Even if you have a vegetable bed, plant up containers to bring crops closer to the kitchen.

May: what to sow

READY FOR WINTER
Maincrop carrots, such as 'Autumn King' and 'Flyaway', are slower to mature than early varieties. Sow them now until midsummer for crops to store. Sow seed thinly into 1cm (½in) deep drills, spaced 15cm (6in) apart, then thin to 5–8cm (2–3in). Choose well-dug soil in full sun that is not stony or recently manured.

HARVEST: **JUL–DEC**

SOW SQUASH
Summer and winter squash can be sown outside next month but it's worth giving crops a head start in cooler areas. Sow seed 2cm (¾in) deep into small pots or modules, in a heated propagator or on a warm windowsill. Water lightly to prevent damping off.

HARVEST: **VARIOUS**

SOW

SWEDES & TURNIPS

MAINCROP CARROTS

SALSIFY

GARDEN SQUASH

ROOTS TO SUCCESS
HARVEST: **VARIOUS**

Sow swedes and turnips 1cm (½in) deep in drills, into good soil that stays moist to help prevent them becoming tough.

SWEDES
Slower-maturing and larger growing than turnips, thin the developing swede plants to 25cm (10in) apart. Harvest in autumn.

TURNIPS
Fast-growing, sow early varieties now for a midsummer crop. Sow maincrop varieties in midsummer for an autumn and winter crop.

CURIOUS SALSIFY
This unusual root crop has an earthy, nutty flavour, and can be boiled or steamed. It grows in any soil that is not too stony. On heavier soil, dig a trench to a spade's depth, and fill it with sandy soil or compost to help the long roots develop. Rake the soil to a fine tilth and sow seed thinly in rows 30cm (12in) apart. Germination can be slow, but thin seedlings to about 15cm (6in) apart.

HARVEST: **NOV–MAY**

STILL TIME TO SOW

You can still sow most crops from last month, indoors and out, if you've had a slow start. Now is your last chance to sow sprouting broccoli, French and runner beans, and sweet corn.

YEAR-ROUND LEAVES

The closely related leaf crops Swiss chard and leaf beet are very easy to grow, and can be enjoyed raw in salads or cooked. They are a good choice for smaller gardens. Protect the plants during winter, and you can look forward to fresh greens even in the coldest months.

HARVEST: ALL YEAR

1 PREPARE THE SITE
Neither crop is fussy about the site, but they both prefer soil that has been improved with plenty of well-rotted manure.

2 SOW IN DRILLS
The seeds of these crops are large and easy to handle. Sow them thinly in drills 2cm (¾in) deep and spaced 38cm (15in) apart.

3 COVER AND WATER
Carefully cover the seeds and water them well. Swiss chard can also be sown singly in modules and planted out later.

4 THIN SEEDLINGS
As they grow, thin individual plants to 30cm (12in) apart. Don't waste the thinned young plants, use them in your salads.

CABBAGE & CAULIFLOWER

WITLOOF & SUGARLOAF CHICORY

SWISS CHARD & LEAF BEET

WINTER BRASSICAS

Now is the time to sow your winter cabbages and spring cauliflowers, so they have time to grow before the cold, frosty weather comes. Sow outdoors into a seedbed, 1cm (½in) deep in drills. Grow them on, thinning the young plants to 8–10cm (3–4in) apart, then transplant them into their final positions in July. Avoid planting cauliflowers on freshly manured soil, which promotes excess leafy growth.

HARVEST: VARIOUS

CHIC CHICORY

For Witloof chicory to force in winter, and summer and autumn crops of sugarloaf varieties, sow from now to early summer. Witloof chicory prefers poor soil, sugarloaf-types need rich soil. Sow both 1cm (½in) deep, in drills 30cm (12in) apart, thinning to 25cm (10in). Sugarloaf can also be sown into modules for transplanting.

HARVEST: VARIOUS

May: what to plant

YOUNG CELERY

Young self-blanching and trench celery plants, sown in February, can now be hardened off and planted out, once the risk of frost has passed. Celery needs rich, moist soil in full sun to do well. Self-blanching types are often planted in blocks to keep the stems upright, so space plants about 20cm (8in) apart. For trench celery, work manure or compost into a 30cm (12in) deep and 45cm (18in) wide trench and fill in to leave a 5cm (2in) dip along the length to retain moisture. Plant the celery in the dip about 30cm (12in) apart.

HARVEST: **AUG–DEC**

FLORENCE FENNEL

Florence fennel, sown earlier in April, should now be full of feathery foliage, ready to be hardened off and planted out. If the weather is still chilly wait a little longer, or the plants will bolt (run to seed). Florence fennel needs a good moist soil, so work in plenty of compost before planting. Allow space for the swelling stems: about 30cm (12in), between each plant. Water them in well and watch out for snails and slugs.

HARVEST: **JUN–OCT**

BROCCOLI   CELERY   LEEKS   FLORENCE FENNEL

PLANT

BIG BRASSICAS

Brussels sprouts, which crop autumn to winter, and sprouting broccoli, to pick in spring, are tall, wide plants and need to be planted in a firm soil to give their roots a good hold and stop them toppling over. Transplant them from their seedbed when the plants are 8–10cm (3–4in) tall. Space broccoli and dwarf Brussels sprout varieties 60cm (24in) apart and tall sprout types 90cm (36in) apart.

HARVEST: **VARIOUS**

LARGE LEEKS

If you want large leeks, dig in plenty of compost before planting. Seedlings sown under cover should be hardened off and planted out when they are 15–20cm (6–8in) tall. Space them 15cm (6in) apart and allow 30cm (12in) between rows. To plant, make a 15cm (6in) deep hole with a dibber, pop in a leek and water each row as you finish.

HARVEST: **SEPT–APR**

PLANTING PLUGS

Many vegetable varieties can be bought as small plants from garden centres or as plug plants from mail order nurseries. These are a great way to fill your vegetable plot if you have limited time or no space to raise tender crops indoors. Choose stocky, dark green plants.

HARVEST: **VARIOUS**

1 UNPACK THE PLUGS
If you bought your plug plants through mail order, you should unpack them, plant,and water them as soon as they arrive.

2 PLANT CAREFULLY
If you are planting outside, dig a hole for each plantlet and drop it in. Plug plants need to be hardened off, so protect them at night.

3 MULCH AROUND
After the first watering, put a layer of mulch around each seedling. This helps to hold warmth and moisture in the soil.

4 KEEP WELL WATERED
Keep the young plants well watered for 2 weeks or so, while they establish, and protect them against slugs and snails.

PLUG PLANTS

SQUASH & PUMPKINS

TOMATOES

WINTER SQUASH & PUMPKINS   HARVEST: **SEPT–OCT**

These vigorous trailing plants need 3–4 months of warm weather to produce a worthwhile crop.

1 SLIDE FROM POT
Squash and pumpkin seedlings are ready when they have three or four true leaves. Ease the plants gently out of their pots.

2 DIG LARGE HOLE
Plant in rich soil at least 1m (3ft) apart, using a trowel to dig a fairly large hole for each seedling. Firm them in and water well.

START TOMATOES

Plant up tomatoes into the greenhouse border, growing bags, or large containers. Bush varieties are attractive for windowsills and conservatories. Tall cordon varieties can be grown indoors, too, if there is enough space and light. Plant them 45cm (18in) apart, or two per growing bag ,and add canes or twine supports to the apex of the greenhouse immediately, because growth is rapid.

HARVEST: **JUL–OCT**

May: more to plant

SUN-LOVING AUBERGINES

Aubergines love warmth and are difficult to grow in temperate climates. The plants are best kept under cover, either in a greenhouse or conservatory, or on a windowsill. Pot them up into 20cm (8in) pots in potting compost, or plant them in the greenhouse border 30–40cm (12–16in) apart, allowing them as much light as possible. If you live in a very mild area and have a sheltered spot outdoors, a dwarf variety of aubergine such as 'Bambino' will fruit successfully in a good summer.

HARVEST: **AUG–OCT**

YOUNG CELERIAC

Although mature celeriac plants are extremely hardy, seedlings will bolt (run to seed) if exposed to low temperatures. Don't harden them off until the weather is mild. Plant out celeriac seedlings 30cm (12in) apart in soil that has been enriched with organic matter so that it retains plenty of moisture. Water the young plants well after planting and continue to water them regularly to help swell the roots.

HARVEST: **OCT–MAR**

PLANT

AUBERGINES

CELERIAC

CABBAGE

COURGETTES

PLANT OUT CABBAGE

When your summer and autumn cabbages, sown in March, are about 8cm (3in) tall, transplant them into their final positions. Ideally, choose a sunny bed with firm soil. Space summer cabbages about 35cm (14in) apart and autumn-types (20in) 50cm apart. Make holes using a dibber, and lift plants into them gently by the leaves not the stem. Firm the soil around the roots and water well.

HARVEST: **AUG–NOV**

COURGETTES

If you have enough space in a greenhouse or polytunnel, plant courgettes into soil improved with compost or well-rotted manure for an early crop. These plants are large and very hungry and thirsty, so space them at least 90cm (36in) apart. A fabric mulch helps to retain moisture.

HARVEST: **JUL–OCT**

LATE EARLIES
Maincrop potato varieties are usually planted at this time of year, but if you have limited space and are looking for a quicker crop, then there's nothing to stop you planting an early variety, as long as you can find seed potatoes this late in the season. Make drills 15cm (6in) deep and plant maincrops 38cm (15in) apart with the chitting end pointing upwards, leaving 75cm (30in) between rows. Allow 30cm (12in) between earlies, with rows at least 38cm (15in) apart. Cover over with soil and water if it is dry.

HARVEST: **AUG–SEP**

CLIMBING CROPS
Once melon and indoor cucumber plants, sown in April, have two or three leaves, plant them into a greenhouse border, 45cm (18in) apart, or two per growing bag. Don't plant deeply, because stems are prone to neck rot. Water well, keep moist, and shade the leaves from hot scorching sun. Provide support.

HARVEST: **VARIOUS**

POTATOES

MELONS & CUCUMBERS

PEPPERS

PLANT OUT PEPPERS
HARVEST: **JUL–OCT**

Peppers and chillies thrive under cover, giving earlier, larger crops than plants grown outside. Plant in pots, growing bags, or ideally in a greenhouse border.

1 WHEN AND WHERE
Peppers and chillies are large enough to plant into a border once they have their first flowers. Make sure the bed is free-draining.

2 SETTING OUT
Ease plants from their pots, handling the rootball not the stem or leaves. Position them in rows, 30–45cm (12–18in) apart.

3 FIRM IN AND WATER
Bury the plants at the same depths as in their pots, and firm them in gently. Water them well, and don't allow them to dry out.

TAKE NOTE

On bright, sunny days, greenhouses and cold frames can become very warm. Open vents and windows, and ensure your plants and seedlings don't dry out.

May: what to do

DOUBLE FRUIT CROP

Removing every other fruit from your gooseberry bushes in the second half of this month will give you a crop of smaller berries to cook now and allow the remaining fruit to develop to an impressive size for harvesting in June. This practice is worthwhile only for dessert gooseberries that are going to be eaten uncooked.

SPOTLESS STRAWBERRIES

As the fruit begins to swell on strawberry plants, apply a mulch around them, tucking it right under the berries to keep them clean and away from the soil.

STRAWBERRY MAT
Fibre strawberry mats or collars that fit neatly around the plants are an easy way of protecting the fruit.

PLASTIC SHEET
Cut holes in plastic sheeting for the plants to grow through. Keep the sheet taut to avoid water pooling.

STRAW BEDDING
The traditional strawberry mulch is a thick layer of straw. Pack it carefully beneath each plant.

TEND

GOOSEBERRIES

RASPBERRIES

YOUNG PLANTS

STRAWBERRIES

CUTTING CANES

Raspberries are vigorous plants that send up new canes from their base each spring. Summer-fruiting types can become overcrowded, which may lead to a poor and possibly diseased crop. Thin them out by removing the weakest of this year's shoots, leaving five or six strong new canes per plant. Pull out new canes that spring up away from the row, to check unwanted spreading.

STILL DELICATE

Even when hardened off, seedlings are vulnerable to late frosts. If there is a cold snap, plant out under cloches or tunnels covered with fleece. Old newspapers make good overnight cover if frost is forecast. Soft new growth is also vulnerable to pests: keep bugs out with barriers such as netting, fleece, or brassica collars.

PINCH OUT TOMATOES

Tomatoes grow rapidly once planted in their final positions and if you have chosen tall cordon (indeterminate) varieties, such as 'Gardener's Delight' or 'Shirley', they will soon need some support. As they race upwards, regularly tie the main stems loosely on to their canes or stakes with twine. At the same time, remove any sideshoots that are developing where the leaves branch from the main stem. Vigorous shoots are often sent up from the base of the plant and these should be removed, too.

BEAT THE BUGS

Cover crops with fleece or net immediately after planting to keep out pests such as carrot fly. Buy or make rigid wire hoops to support the netting. and push them into the soil, covering the row, every 30cm (12in). Lay the netting over the hoops and anchor it into the soil with metal pegs or weight it down with lengths of wood.

TOMATOES

PROTECT CROPS

GREENHOUSES

SCORCHING HOT

In a greenhouse, intense summer sun can scorch the foliage of plants and raise the temperature far too high. Put up shading in late spring and remove it in early autumn as the sun's strength diminishes. Blinds are expensive, but there are many cheaper options.

PAINT-ON SHADING
Shading paint is cheap and is easy to apply to the outside of glass greenhouses. It will not wipe off some plastics, so check the label.

SHADING MESH
Shading fabric may not look particularly attractive, but when attached to the outside of the greenhouse it is highly effective.

EFFECTIVE VENTILATION
Leave doors and vents open all day if it is very hot. Automatic ventilators are available that open and close vents according to temperature.

DAMPING DOWN
Sprinkle water on floors and staging to stop the atmosphere becoming too dry. Shut doors and vents for a while afterwards to increase the humidity.

May: what to harvest

PEAK TIME FOR HERBS
Annual herbs sown in April, and perennial ones planted last autumn, should be ready for the kitchen in the next few weeks. Many herbs need pinching out now to encourage bushy growth, so take advantage and use the shoots in your cooking. Most of the soft new growth should be tender enough to pinch off between your fingers, but scissors are better for woodier plants like rosemary and some thymes, and neater for chives. Pick the large leaves of basil as required and pinch out the flower shoots as they come.

SALAD SEASON
Sown outside in April, now is the start of the main lettuce season, with non-hearting, loose-leaf varieties, such as 'Green Salad Bowl' and 'Catalogna', ready first. To keep them cropping over several weeks, pick off the outer leaves as required, or cut the leaves with scissors about 2.5cm (1in) from the soil and allow them to re-sprout. Hearting types follow, which can be pulled up by the roots or cut at the base with a knife.

HARVEST

GOOSEBERRIES HERBS LETTUCE

GALLERY OF GOOSEBERRIES
Gooseberries harvested this month are likely to be acidic, so perfect for cooking. Fruit left to ripen will soften and yellow, signalling that they are sweet enough to eat raw. Unless you have thornless variety, watch out for the fearsome spines when picking the fruit.

'HINNOMAKI RED'
Slow-growing variety that produces a heavy crop of large fruit that ripen red. It has good resistance to mildew. Good for small gardens.

'HINNOMAKI YELLOW'
A strong variety that bears a good yield of large, sweet, yellow fruit. It also shows good mildew resistance. Dessert variety, it's good eaten raw.

'INVICTA'
Widely available, this reliable dual-purpose variety can be eaten straight from the bush or cooked. It has good mildew resistance.

'CAPTIVATOR'
An almost thornless variety, good for gardens with children. It's sweet fruit ripen red and can be eaten from the bush. Good mildew resistance.

ASPARAGUS CROWNS

If you have planted asparagus crowns this year, patience is the order of the day. To allow plants to become established and build up strength, leave spears uncut in their first and second seasons. In subsequent years harvest the spears when they reach around 15cm (6in) tall, cutting them with a sharp knife, 5cm (2in) below the soil surface. Harvest them over a period of 6 weeks but leave at least six strong spears per plant to grow on. These will supply the all-important energy for the following year's crop.

ROOT TREATS

It's a real treat this month to be able to harvest the first salad beetroot and baby carrots, sown in March. Do this carefully, loosening heavy soils with a hand fork first to avoid damaging the roots, especially carrots. Twist rather than cut the leaves off your beetroot to prevent them bleeding. Remember, their leaves are good to eat, too.

TURNIPS

ASPARAGUS

BROAD BEANS

BEETROOT & CARROTS

TENDER TURNIPS

There's no denying that turnips are a quick crop to grow. Early varieties can be ready for harvest in just 6–7 weeks after sowing, so make sure you catch them at their best – while they're still sweet and tender. For perfect baby turnips, pull them when they are less than 5cm (2in) in diameter. If left to grow much larger, they soon become tough and unappetizing.

BROAD APPEAL

Broad beans sown in autumn or late winter should start to yield fleece-lined pods full of delicious, sweet beans this month. Pick frequently, because the beans are at their best when small and tender. If you've a glut, harvest the beans small and freeze them. Don't leave them to become big and starchy.

Organic pest control

Every garden, no matter how well tended, will have its share of pests and diseases to contend with. When you are growing your own food, you may prefer not to spray crops with pesticides. Instead, try for natural biological control by encouraging, or introducing, populations of beneficial creatures to prey on persistent pests.

Grow healthy plants

Regularly maintaining your kitchen garden helps minimize problems with pests and diseases. Constantly improving the soil with plenty of organic matter will improve its structure and fertility, and allow plants to grow stronger, making them more resistant to infection and damage. Keeping beds free of plant debris and weeds is also good practice, leaving pests and diseases with nowhere to hide or overwinter, so tidy the area you're cultivating regularly. Keep an eye out for the first signs of pests, such as aphids on shoot tips, and tackle them before you have an infestation on your hands. Simply squashing greenfly or small caterpillars can be remarkably effective.

Friendly predators

Providing food, water, and shelter for a wide range of wildlife will encourage them into your garden, where they will feed on pests and help keep their numbers under control. Feeders will bring in birds that also have a taste for aphids, caterpillars, snails, and other pests. Hedgehogs devour slugs, snails, and grubs of all kinds, so are worth encouraging with piles of logs and leaves. Where an insect pest does take hold, it's possible to introduce a biological control, such as nematodes, to combat them.

APPLY NEMATODES
Microscopic, parasitic nematode worms effectively control a range of pests, including slugs, snails, caterpillars, and weevils. They come in a powder, which is watered into the soil using a watering can.

GROW FLOWERS
Growing flowers among your crops not only adds colour, but also encourages pollinating insects to visit. These often feed on pests, too. The scent of flowers may also prevent pests locating crops.

CREATE HABITATS
Creating different habitats entices all kinds of beneficial creatures to take up residence. A pond will bring frogs, toads, and insects, as well as other hungry and thirsty animals and birds.

MAKE HIDING PLACES
Hiding places, such as log piles, pieces of old carpet, or propped up slates, provide shelter for beneficial creatures like hedgehogs and frogs. If you find pests sheltering too, just remove them.

BENEFICIAL BUGS

Many insects pollinate crops and some feed voraciously on common insect pests, so it's a good idea to make your garden attractive to them.

Lacewings – Larvae and adults feast on aphids and other insect pests. Attract them with nectar-rich flowers.

Ladybirds – Adults and larvae prey on aphids. Provide dry places, such as seedpods, for them to overwinter.

Hoverflies – These wasp look-a-likes devour aphids and pollinate crops. Encourage them with colourful flowers.

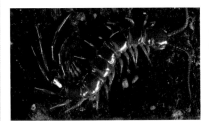

Centipede – At home in leaf litter and log piles, centipedes have an eager appetite for all kinds of insect pests.

Sacrificial planting – Grow plants that pests can't resist, to distract them from crops, or to alert you to the problem so you can control it. For example, blackfly love nasturtiums.

ORGANIC PEST CONTROL

June: what to sow

LATER LETTUCE

Sow now for late-summer and autumn crops. Choose cos, butterhead, or crisphead-types for hearted lettuce; loose-leaf varieties to crop as cut leaves. In hot weather, lettuce might fail to germinate or wilt once growing. Sow in lightly shaded beds, and if the weather is very hot, sow in the evenings and cool the soil first with water.

HARVEST: **JUL–NOV**

SOW AND SOW

Don't forget to continue sowing cut-and-come-again salad crops for a constant supply. A range of baby leaf crops are suitable. Weed the soil and sow seed thinly in drills, 10–15cm (4–6in) wide, to give a mass of foliage to cut in a few weeks time.

HARVEST: **ALL YEAR**

SOW

EDIBLE FLOWERS   LETTUCE   CHINESE GREENS   CUT & COME AGAIN

BLOOMING TASTY

HARVEST: JUL–OCT

Annual flowers are often overlooked in the productive garden, but many are edible as well as beautiful, and have their own distinct flavour. Direct sow now.

CALENDULA
Also known as pot marigold, this cheerful plant flowers in shades of yellow and orange. Use the petals to add colour to your salads.

NASTURTIUM
The leaves, flowers, and seed pods of this colourful, spreading plant have a delicious but strong peppery taste. It is best used sparingly.

FRENCH MARIGOLD
This summer bedding plant has a very pungent flavour. Use the flowers in salads, and add the petals to rice dishes for colour and a spicy kick.

FAR EAST FEAST

Chinese cabbage and pak choi like warmth, so wait until this month to sow, when they will be less likely to bolt. Both need moist, fertile soil, and will tolerate light shade. Sow seed thinly in drills 30cm (12in) apart for Chinese cabbage, 25cm (10in) for pak choi. Repeat sow, thin seedlings, and harvest in 6–8 weeks, when ready.

HARVEST: **JUL–NOV**

HURRY NOW FOR HERBS

HARVEST: **JUL–OCT**

This is the last chance to sow most annual herbs. If you leave it any later, they rapidly run to seed at the expense of the leaves you want for the kitchen.

1 SOWING OUTDOORS
Sow tougher herbs, such as dill, parsley, and coriander, directly into the soil outside in rows or patches. Space evenly.

2 GROWING ON
Keep the seed well watered and thin the seedlings to 20cm (8in) apart as they develop. Protect from slugs and snails.

SOWING INDOORS
In all but the mildest areas, sow basil indoors, grow it on undercover, and plant it out in a few weeks time.

STILL TIME TO SOW

Sow outside now: peas, kohl rabi, turnips, sprouting broccoli, beetroot, calabrese, Florence fennel, kale, carrots, sugarloaf and Witloof chicory, and chard.

SQUASHES & CUCUMBERS

FRENCH & RUNNER BEANS

ANNUAL HERBS

SQUASH FAMILY

With the last frosts now past, summer cucumbers and courgettes can be sown under cloches in their final positions outside, as can summer and winter squashes, and pumpkins. All need a sunny site, sheltered from the wind, and soil that has been improved with plenty of well-rotted manure or compost. Sow two seeds per station, 2.5cm (1in) deep, spaced 90cm (3ft) apart for cucumbers and courgettes, and at least 1.5m (5ft) apart for squashes and pumpkins.

HARVEST: **VARIOUS**

LATE BEANS

For late crops of French and runner beans, sow now, directly into soil prepared with plenty of rich organic matter. If you're growing climbing varieties, remember to put the supports in first. Sow two seeds per station, 5cm (2in) deep, 15–20cm (6–8in) apart. Thin out the weaker plant.

HARVEST: **AUG–OCT**

June: what to plant

PLANT CAULIFLOWER

Spring-sown summer and autumn cauliflower should be ready to transplant from their seedbed now. Using a dibber, lift the seedlings carefully and transplant them into fertile soil that hasn't been manured recently. Space 60cm (24in) apart in each direction and water well and net them where pigeons are a problem.

HARVEST: **AUG–NOV**

PLANT GREENS

It's now time to plant out kale and sprouting broccoli, sown in spring. Both crops grow outside through winter, so give them shelter, and soil that hasn't been dug recently, to help their roots anchor securely. Transplant them from their seedbed in the same way as cauliflowers.

HARVEST: **DEC–APR**

PLANT

CAULIFLOWER

KALE & BROCCOLI

AUBERGINES

SUGARLOAF CHICORY

AUBERGINES, PEPPERS, & TOMATOES

HARVEST: **JUL–OCT**

Once plants raised indoors have been hardened off, and have their first flowers showing, these heat-loving crops can be planted outside in sunny, sheltered spots.

AUBERGINES
Aubergines give a better harvest when planted into large containers. Keep them well fed and watered. Harvest August – October.

PEPPERS
Plant in beds, containers, or grow bags, in full sun, and support with canes. They need good light and warmth to ripen fully.

TOMATOES
Suitable for beds, pots, or growing bags. All upright varieties require staking with canes. Grow cordon varieties under cover. Crop from July.

PLANT CHICORY

Sown last month, plant out your sugarloaf chicory seedlings now. This type of chicory forms dense heads that are larger than other forms, and they appreciate soil that has had compost dug into it recently, to encourage leafy growth. Harden off the plants and space them out evenly at 25cm (10in) intervals. Water in well.

HARVEST: **JUL–OCT**

FAMILY FRUIT

HARVEST: **JUL–OCT**

These related crops are hungry plants, so work in plenty of compost when you plant out, once hardened off. Cover with cloches if the weather is cool and damp.

COURGETTE

These are large, quick-growing plants that need plenty of space. Position them 90cm (36in) apart. Can also be grown in large pots.

CUCUMBER

This crop is usually trained upwards on canes, and can be grown in large containers. Keep them well watered and ventilated.

SQUASH

Summer squash crop from July, winter varieties from September. Grow them vertically up canes where space is limited.

DON'T FORGET

When planting out, always water plants in well, and continue to keep them moist during dry spells.

Water under cloches regularly and prop them open to allow air to cool plants on sunny days.

CUCUMBERS, COURGETTES, & SQUASH

SWEET CORN

FRENCH & RUNNER BEANS

SWEET CORN

HARVEST: **SEP–OCT**

If your plants are hardened off, plant out now in a sheltered spot, into good soil that doesn't dry out.

PLANTING OUT

Sweet corn doesn't do well if its growth is checked, so plant while the young plants are still small. Water thoroughly before planting.

WORK IN BLOCKS

Pollination is vital for full cobs, so plant in blocks with plants 45cm (18in) apart each way. This makes wind pollination more effective.

SUMMMER BEANS

Batches of French and runner beans, raised under cover in pots or modules, can be planted out as soon as their supports are in place. Plant one per cane, or space them out 15–20cm (6–8in) apart along rows of netting or wire. Dwarf varieties require a similar spacing, but no supports. Try planting sweet peas to cling alongside runner beans to help attract pollinating insects.

HARVEST: **AUG–OCT**

June: what to do

SUMMER PRUNING
This is a quick job that is worth carrying out after gooseberries, redcurrants, and whitecurrants have been harvested. Prune all of this year's new growth back to five leaves, cutting with sharp secateurs just above a leaf. Removing the tips of soft new growth stops the plants being colonized by aphids or infected with mildew and opens up the bush to improve airflow.

WATER AND HOE
Container-grown plants need frequent watering in hot weather, but so do plants in the soil. Keep an eye on plants that are prone to bolting and soak them well, perhaps once a week. Hoe between crops to remove weeds, leaving them to shrivel and die.

TEND

FRUIT BUSHES

MAINTENANCE

TOMATOES

SUMMER BERRIES

KEEP UP THE SUPPORT
Your tomatoes will still be heading skywards, so continue to tie them in to sturdy stakes or wires and pinch out sideshoots.

1 REMOVE SIDESHOOTS
Pinch out sideshoots that form where leaves join the main stem, because they will take energy away from flowering and fruiting.

2 TIE LOOSELY
When you attach the main stem of a tomato plant to its support, tie the twine loosely to allow the stem to expand.

CANE CONTROL
New canes sent up this year from the base of summer-fruiting raspberry and blackberry plants will now be getting long and unruly. Tie them in to keep them out of the way and prevent them getting damaged. The older canes that will fruit this year should be spread across the supporting wires, so keep the new shoots close together for now and spread them out once the older canes have been cut back.

WATCH THEM CLIMB

As they grow, climbing varieties of French and runner beans twist their stems around their supporting canes. Once established, they can hang on tightly without your help. Sometimes, however, seedlings need a hand to get started, especially if they are getting tossed around in breezy conditions or flattened by heavy rain. Once the young plants are tall enough, tie each one loosely onto its support with garden twine, taking care not to damage the delicate stem, then watch them take off without tangling.

TRIM HERBS

Many shrubby and perennial herbs, such as rosemary, sage, and thyme, finish flowering during early summer, which gives you the opportunity to cut them back and keep them tidy. Trimming also encourages new growth that will quickly be ready to harvest. Use secateurs or shears depending on the size of the job.

STRAWBERRIES

RUNNER BEANS

HERBS

NEW PLANTS FROM OLD

Strawberry plants are easy to propagate from the long runners that they all produce. At no extra cost, you can increase your stock and replace old plants.

1 CHOOSE RUNNERS
Choose four or five strong runners and cut off the rest. Also remove runners from plants you don't want to use for propagation.

2 PEG DOWN IN POTS
Set the runners in buried pots of compost and peg down with wire. Once the plantlets have grown on, cut the runners and plant out.

3 PROPAGATE IN SOIL
You can also let the runners grow directly in the soil. Reposition the plantlet if necessary, peg it down and sever when established.

DON'T FORGET

The weeks that follow are likely to be hot and dry. If you haven't already laid an organic mulch around your plants to conserve moisture, do it now.

June: more to do

EARTH UP MAINCROPS
When maincrop potatoes reach about 20cm (8in) tall, earth them up by pulling soil around their stems, leaving the top leaves showing. This not only prevents tubers turning green and inedible in the light, it can help protect them from the spores of potato blight. This fungal disease thrives in warm, wet summers. Look for brown patches at leaf edges, and remove and destroy infected growth.

REGULAR MEALS
Whether your tomatoes, peppers, chillies, and aubergines are grown in the soil or in containers, they need regular feeding once the first fruit begins to set. Apply a high-potash tomato fertilizer every week. Use a sunken pot to help deliver the feed straight to the roots.

TEND

POTATOES

FRUIT BUSHES

SOFT FRUIT

TOMATOES

MILDEW ALERT
If powdery white patches appear on your gooseberry and blackcurrant bushes, it probably means they have been infected with American gooseberry mildew. This fungal disease particularly affects young growth, which becomes misshapen and dies. The mildew also appears on the fruits, which are still edible, though unappealing. Gooseberry mildew thrives in environments where air circulation is poor. The best control is to remove and destroy affected leaves and fruits, and prune the bushes to thin out growth and allow free air circulation.

PROTECT SOFT FRUIT
Birds love ripe, soft summer fruits as much as we do. To stop them feasting on your crops of berries and currants, protect the fruit with netting. The easiest way to do this is to plant bushes together and build a permanent fruit cage around them, but this is not always practical in smaller gardens. To net individual bushes, drive in four stakes around each one to hold up the net. Cover them over before the fruit ripens and changes colour. Ensure that the net is weighted down at the edges, because birds are adept at getting in and can easily become trapped.

SPOT CHECK FOR PESTS

Spotting pests early, before they have a chance to multiply and damage crops, is key to keeping problems under control. Check under leaves as you pass, and if plants are unexpectedly wilting, try digging one up to look for pests that attack the roots.

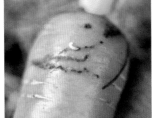

BLACKFLY
These aphids can rapidly smother foliage, sucking the sap and excreting a sticky substance that causes a black mould to develop.

CARROT FLY
The white maggots of this fly will destroy your carrot crop. Protect your plants with fine netting to prevent the female fly from laying her eggs.

ASPARAGUS BEETLE
Both the brightly coloured adult beetles and their dark grey larvae rapidly strip asparagus stems. Pick them off by hand and destroy them.

ONION FLY
The maggots feed on the roots and bulbs of onions. Signs are yellow, collapsing plants. Onion sets are less vulnerable than seedlings.

PESTS

APPLES & PEARS

BROAD BEANS

THE JUNE DROP

Many apple and pear trees shed fruitlets in late June or early July. This 'June drop' may alarm first-time fruit growers, but it is the tree's way of ditching unhealthy fruit and leaving a smaller crop that is easier for it to carry. Do your own thinning after the June drop for a crop of large, healthy fruit, especially on young trees that need to make plenty of strong growth too.

BEAN TOPS

Young shoots at the top of broad bean plants are a magnet for blackfly. Infestation can be pre-empted by pinching out the soft tips of these shoots between your fingers when the plants are in full flower. This also helps direct the plant's energy into swelling the beans rather than producing more leaves.

June: what to harvest

TASTE OF SUMMER
June is the peak month for strawberries, when early varieties, like 'Honeoye', bear fruit. Pick berries with their hulls attached, when fully ripe and entirely red. Fruit will ripen every day or two, so keep picking them at their best. Eat fresh, or use in jams or cordials.

CUT ARTICHOKES
Globe artichokes are ready to cut now. Cut them young if you like them tightly closed and tender, or let them mature more if you prefer a fuller flavour. Don't leave them too long or they become hard and inedible. Planted in April, fully mature specimens will often produce a second flush of flowerheads in late summer.

HARVEST

STRAWBERRIES

GLOBE ARTICHOKE

PEAS

FLORENCE FENNEL

PEAS OFFERING
Peas are at their best for a short time, and should be picked often and eaten soon, before their sweetness fades. Pluck the pods of shelling peas when they look full, but not solid, and are still bright green. Mangetout varieties snap cleanly in half at their prime, but might still need strings removing from pods. When the harvest is over, cut the plants down, leaving the nitrogen-rich roots in the soil.

FIRST FENNEL
Harvest Florence fennel once the bulbs reach a useful size. Either cut them with a knife as close to soil level as possible, or cut 2.5cm (1in) above the soil, leaving the stump. Crops sown in April may give a second flush of flavoursome shoots. Don't forget, the ferny leaves pack a delicious aniseed punch, too.

VEGETABLE FEAST

Pull kohl rabi and turnips, sown in spring, once they reach the size of a golf ball. Maincrop turnips are good to eat when much larger, but early varieties can become woody. Pak choi is often ready just 6 weeks after sowing, when it can be uprooted or cut about 2.5cm (1in) from the base and left to grow back. Calabrese and the first summer cauliflowers are also ready to harvest now, and mature rapidly. Cut the heads while the buds are tightly closed. Split surplus heads into florets for freezing.

BULB BOUNTY

Planted in autumn, garlic is usually dug in August, but uproot some now for juicy bulbs, milder than any in the shops, and use immediately. Garlic bulbs can grow deep in the soil, so lift them with a fork. Overwintered onion varieties, planted last year, will also be ready to harvest now. Loosen the soil at their roots and lift as required.

NEW POTATOES

BRASSICAS

GARLIC & ONIONS

TASTY NEW POTATOES

Harvest new potatoes when the plants flower, loosening the soil with a fork. Lift all the tubers – any left may sprout and encourage disease.

'FOREMOST'
Good for salads, boiling and baking, this first-year variety is white-skinned, and has an excellent waxy texture.

'RED DUKE OF YORK'
A good all-rounder in the kitchen, this variety has a red skin, yellow flesh, and a dry texture. It also has a wonderfully strong flavour.

'INTERNATIONAL KIDNEY'
This is the variety widely sold in supermarkets as 'Jersey Royal'. Best boiled, it has a waxy texture and delicious, yellow flesh.

DON'T FORGET

Check your new potatoes are ready to harvest by scraping away soil from the base of the plants to reveal the tubers. If they look small, cover them again and give them longer to grow.

Space efficiency

However large your plot, you'll want to make the most of the space. This could be as simple as finding gaps in the flower border for fruit and vegetables, but by planting fast-growing crops, you can squeeze extra harvests out of the vegetable plot as well. Sow them in empty soil that is waiting for the next crop to be planted (catch-cropping), or grow them between slow-maturing plants (inter-cropping).

Catch-cropping

Even with meticulous planning it's inevitable that sometimes you will be left with bare soil during the growing season – after one long-term crop is harvested and before the next is ready to plant. This gives you an opportunity to sow a fast-growing crop that will use the space in the meantime, and will finish in plenty of time to prepare the ground in readiness for the crop to follow.

Catch-cropping is particularly useful to fill the gap between winter brassicas, the last of which are often picked in early spring, and tender summer crops that

(left to right) **The last early potatoes** are lifted in summer, leaving the bed temporarily empty. **Sow radish next**, to harvest in 6–8 weeks, just in time to make way for new spring cabbage seedlings, transplanted from their bed.

can't usually be planted outdoors until towards the end of May. Another lull may come between lifting early potatoes and planting spring cabbages in late summer. Keep a stock of seeds handy of quick-growing crops that are ready to harvest in 6–8 weeks, such as radishes, beetroot, and pak choi, right through the growing season and your plot will always be full.

Inter-cropping

Effective inter-cropping takes advantage of the fact that some crops are quicker growing than others, and that they can be grown closely together without competing. Slow-growing crops, such as Brussels sprouts and parsnips, take months to mature, locking up your beds for long periods. In contrast, turnips and beetroots are ready to harvest in just 8–10 weeks, so it's a good idea to make use of their speedy growth. To achieve multiple crops from the same bed, water and feed the plants regularly, and try not to disturb your maincrop plants.

1 MAINCROP FIRST
Plant out maincrop vegetables, such as sweet corn, into their final positions. Firm them in and water well. Insert any stakes at this stage to avoid damaging the intercrops later.

2 SOW INTERCROPS
Make seed drills in between the young maincrop vegetables, and sow intercrops directly. Sow later crops around the developing maincrop to prevent them from being shaded.

TRY THESE

Inter-cropping and catch-cropping requires fruit and vegetables that mature quickly, to avoid interrupting the cycle of maincrop harvests.

Lettuce can be harvested as leaves in a matter of weeks. If time allows between crops, let them form heads.

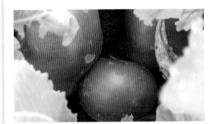

Turnips can be ready in just 6 weeks, making them ideal for inter-cropping between onions, shallots, and beans.

Pak choi matures quickly and can also be cut as baby leaves, allowing you to sow new crops until the last minute.

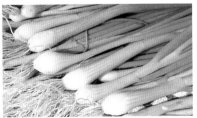

Spring onions are ideal as an extra crop between maincrop onions and shallots, as well as rows of carrots.

Don't let space go to waste in the vegetable plot. In the scheme shown here, courgettes and various fast-growing salad crops have been planted around bean wigwams.

SPACE EFFICIENCY

July: what to sow

BETTER BEETROOT

HARVEST: AUG–OCT

This is your last chance to sow beetroot outdoors for an autumn crop. Choose round varieties, and sow 2cm (¾in) deep, thinning to 10cm (4in).

'RED ACE'
A maincrop variety, it produces dark red roots, and grows well in drier weather without bolting.

'CHIOGGIA PINK'
The plump, red and white striped roots fade to pink when cooked, but are sweet and tender to eat.

'PABLO'
This variety is a good all-rounder that can be grown for early baby roots, as well as autumn crops.

SOW

LATE SEASON PEAS

SPRING CABBAGE & WINTER RADISH

BEETROOT

SOW AUTUMN PEAS

HARVEST: SEP–OCT

Act now, and there's still time go grow a fresh crop of peas in time for autumn. Choose dwarf varieties of shelling-types or mangetout, and sow them direct.

1 PREPARE THE SITE
To avoid summer heat, pick a slightly shaded spot and prepare the soil for planting. You can also use large containers, kept shaded.

2 SOW THE SEED
Sow seed 4cm (1½in) deep in drills, spaced 15–20cm (6–8in) apart. Station-sow in pots at the same depths and distances.

3 GROW THEM ON
Cover the seed with soil and insert pea sticks or plastic netting for support. Keep well watered and tie new growth to supports at first.

COLD SEASON CROPS

There always seems to be a cabbage to sow and this month it's spring varieties, like 'Pixie'. These can be sown in a seedbed, but if space is tight, try sowing them in modules outdoors to plant out later, once mature enough. Large winter radishes should also be sown outside now, 1cm (½in) deep, in drills spaced 30cm (12in) apart. Thin to 15cm (6in) spacing for good-sized roots.

HARVEST: **VARIOUS**

July: what to plant

PLANTING LEEKS OUTSIDE

HARVEST: **DEC–APR**

Late varieties of leek, such as 'Musselburgh', sown in late spring into trays or in a seedbed, should be large enough to plant out. Prepare the site by weeding it thoroughly, and dig in plenty of well-rotted compost to encourage strong, leafy growth.

1 LIFT AND SEPARATE
Carefully lift the young leeks from the seedbed, or tip them from their tray, and separate the roots.

2 PLANT DEEPLY
Leeks need to be planted into holes, 15cm (6in) deep, to give them blanched, white stems. Use a dibber.

3 PROVIDE SPACE
Leave room to grow. Space the plants at 15cm (6in) intervals, in rows 30cm (12in) apart.

4 ALLOW TO SETTLE
Water well but don't firm the soil. Let the holes naturally fill with earth, blanching the stems.

STRAWBERRIES

ENDIVE & WINTER CABBAGE

LEEKS

PLANT

SUMMER BERRIES

Strawberries do well on a free-draining, sunny site, where plenty of well-rotted manure has been added. Avoid beds where strawberries have been grown recently because they're prone to soil-borne diseases. Plant until early autumn for fruit next year, spacing the plants about 45cm (18in) apart, with 75cm (30in) between rows. Position the crown at the base of the leaves level with the soil.

HARVEST: **JUN–SEP**

TASTY LEAVES

Plant out endive and winter cabbage, sown April and May. Both crops like a sunny bed and moist, fertile soil. Space the cabbages 50cm (20in) apart each way, and the endive, 30cm (12in). Cover cabbages with fine net to keep out butterflies. Crop them December – March. Harvest the endive September – March.

HARVEST: **VARIOUS**

July: what to do

EARTH UP BRASSICAS

Lofty winter brassicas, such as purple sprouting broccoli and Brussels sprouts, can be rocked or pulled out of the soil by autumn and winter winds. Now is the time to get them well anchored in the ground, ready for a change in the weather. Draw up soil around the base of their stems and firm it as they grow. In exposed gardens it is worth staking each plant as well.

PINCH OUT

Climbing French and runner beans will keep going upwards for as long as you let them, so pinch out their leading shoots when they reach the top of their supports. This helps divert energy into the production of flowers and beans, and prevents tangled stems.

TEND

BRASSICAS

BEANS

BRASSICA PESTS

TOMATOES

CABBAGE WHITE CAUTION

When you see white butterflies flitting above brassica beds, be sure that they are laying eggs. Only fine netting will keep them out.

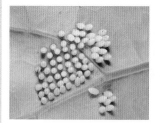

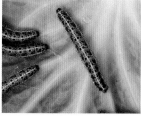

EGGS
Check the undersides of brassica leaves. If you have good eyesight, you will see clusters of the cabbage white butterfly's tiny pale eggs.

CATERPILLARS
Hoards of hungry green or black speckled caterpillars will soon hatch out. Pick them off before they start to devour your crops.

STOP YOUR CORDONS

If you are growing cordon tomatoes, it's time to "stop" them, so they develop fruit rather than leaves. Pinch out the tops of plants when they reach the top of their canes or the apex of the greenhouse. Stop outdoor plants after they have formed four or five trusses of flowers and fruit. Water your plants regularly to help prevent the fruit splitting or developing blossom end rot, right.

TRIM TRAINED TREES

Apple and pear trees that have been trained into cordons, espaliers, or step-overs, need pruning this month. A trim will maintain the shape of the tree and prevent new growth from taking up space needed by the developing fruit. Use clean, sharp secateurs to cut back new shoots coming from the main stem to three leaves from their base. Also cut back shoots arising from existing fruiting spurs or sideshoots to one leaf.

SUMMER TRIM

Acid cherries fruit mostly on shoots formed the previous year, and established trees must be pruned now to encourage new growth for next year. After harvesting, and into early autumn, cut back a quarter of the shoots that bore fruit to a healthy bud near their base. Also cut damaged or unproductive wood from older acid cherry and plum trees.

APRICOT FAN

PRUNE APPLES & PEARS

ACID CHERRIES & PLUMS

SUMMER FAN PRUNING

Summer pruning of established, fan-trained apricots, plums, and cherries is important, because it helps to form fruiting wood for future years.

1 TIE IN
Choose which new shoots you want to grow on for producing fruit and tie them into the fan where they will fill gaps.

2 SHORTEN
Look for new shoots that you don't need to tie in to form part of the framework and shorten them to six leaves from their base.

3 CUT BACK FURTHER
After the fruit has cropped, the untied shoots that you have already shortened need further pruning. Cut them back to three leaves.

DON'T FORGET

If you are going on holiday, ask friends or neighbours to water your plants. Tell them to reward themselves by picking any fruit or vegetables that ripen during your absence.

July: more to do

PEST WATCH

Treat large infestations of aphids on your crops; they can spread cucumber mosaic virus, causing leaves and fruits of cucumbers and courgettes to become blotchy and distorted. Destroy any plants showing symptoms. Also look out for gooseberry sawfly, whitefly, and caterpillars.

TRAIN GRAPE VINES

Vines, grown indoors or out, are commonly trained as cordons, with a single vertical main stem and horizontal laterals that carry flowers and fruit. In summer, pinch out any weak flowers to leave one truss per lateral, then cut each lateral back to two leaves beyond the flower truss. Cut back any lateral without flowers to five leaves, and any sideshoots from the laterals to one leaf. Thin the fruit in each bunch while small.

TEND

INSECT PESTS

GREENHOUSE CROPS

CURLY ENDIVE

GRAPES

DAILY CARE

In a hot summer, greenhouse crops need daily attention. Container plants need watering once a day and feeding with a high-potash fertilizer weekly once the first fruit has set. Good ventilation is also vital to cool the greenhouse and create air movement to help stop fungal diseases. Open all vents and doors fully on hot days, but close them at least partially at night to prevent plants being chilled by low temperatures.

BLANCHING

Blanching whitens and sweetens stems and leaves. Blanch endive when it is mature. Cover the centre with a plate, or put a pot over the whole plant, for about 10 days. With trench celery, either tie the stems loosely with twine and gradually earth them up, or tie a collar around them when the stems are about 30cm (12in) tall.

ENCOURAGE YOUR BEANS

In hot, dry summer weather, runner bean flowers may be less likely to set, which means that no beans will start to form. To help prevent this, give the plants plenty of water at their bases: soak them well at least two or three times a week if the weather is particularly dry. You can also mist the flowers with water using a fine spray. If you have a persistent problem, it's worth experimenting with white-flowered varieties, such as 'White Lady', which seem to set beans more reliably in hot weather.

THIN OUT FRUIT

The natural 'June drop' of fruitlets can continue into July. Once this has finished, continue to thin fruit by hand. On apple trees, remove more of the fruitlets to leave one or two apples per cluster. Pears don't require as much thinning as apples. Thin them once the fruit is pointing downwards, to two fruits per cluster.

WEEDS

RUNNER BEANS

APPLES & PEARS

UNWELCOME PLANTS

Weed your vegetable beds regularly to prevent annual weeds seeding into the soil and the perennials establishing large, hard to remove roots. Hoe between crop rows to destroy weeds as soon as they appear, or use a hand fork to tackle stubborn patches.

HAIRY BITTERCRESS
Long seed pods develop when the flowers of this weed die down. Hairy bittercress is fairly easy to pull out when it is still in early growth.

GOOSEGRASS
Also known as cleavers, this plant has sticky leaves covered with tiny clinging hooks. It spreads rapidly and should be dug up by its roots.

GROUNDSEL
The yellow flowers of this plant develop into fluffy white seed heads like those of dandelions. Root it out before the seeds disperse.

BINDWEED
This persistent creeper and climber can quickly smother crops. It is hard to eliminate, as it can regrow from any fragment of overlooked root.

July: what to harvest

PLENTIFUL BERRIES

Blackberries and summer raspberries will start cropping over the next few weeks, so pick every couple of days. Pick raspberries when they've turned a rich pinky-red, pulling the soft fruit away from the core. Blackberries should be harvested when entirely black and glossy, and often come away with the core still in place. Both fruits keep fresh for only a day or two, so freeze any extra.

CUCUMBERS NOW

Sown in April and grown indoors, the season's first cucumbers will be ready for picking now. Cut the fruit with some stalk, once they are a usable size. Baby fruits are especially delicious. Pick regularly to avoid a glut because cucumbers cannot be stored.

HARVEST

RASPBERRIES

CUCUMBERS

BEANS

CURRANTS

PICK BEANS OFTEN

The secret with French and runner beans is crop often. Pick the pods small and tender for the tastiest crop, which will also help keep the plants productive for longer. French beans that are past their best can be podded for delicious green haricot beans. Whole beans freeze well, if you get overwhelmed, but allow some to develop and ripen fully for seed.

CURRANT CROP

Currants of all colours are cropping this month in abundance. Pick sprigs of red- and whitecurrants whole, as they ripen. Usually, blackcurrants develop over a longer period, so pick the berries individually. Currants don't keep; pick and use them quickly, and freeze any that you can't eat straight away.

PICK COURGETTES AND SUMMER SQUASH

These two crops are closely related and are grown in the same way. They can both be picked when tiny, tender, and at their sweetest, or left to grow larger for stuffing.

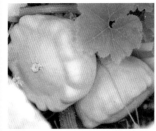

'PATTY PAN'
This variety produces a large crop of saucer-shaped fruit that can be eaten whole when small and young, or allowed to grow on to full-size.

'SUNBURST'
Produces bright yellow fruit that can be harvested as a baby vegetable, or allowed to grow on. They taste delicious when roasted or fried.

'TROMBONCINO'
These elongated fruit can reach up to 1m (3ft) long but are best cut when they reach 30cm (12in). Allow plants to trail or train upwards.

ALSO HARVEST

With lots of fruit and vegetables ready to crop this month, check your broad beans — and don't overlook leafy crops. Harvest pak choi, Chinese cabbage, and red- and sugarloaf chicory until autumn.

COURGETTES & SQUASHES

TOMATOES

ONIONS & SHALLOTS

INDOOR TOMATO TIME

Tomatoes are a sure sign of summer, and the first indoor fruit, sown in spring, are ready to harvest. Pick them as soon as the entire fruit turns red or yellow, depending on variety. Cherry-types should ripen first, followed by salad tomatoes, plum varieties, then the mighty beefsteaks. Pick regularly to encourage a prolonged crop. Best eaten fresh, if you have surplus tomatoes, try oven-drying them.

FIRST ONIONS

Start lifting onions and shallots now as you need them, as soon as they're big enough to use. At this stage the edible leaves should still be green, and the bulbs juicy, with a slightly milder flavour than later, dried harvests. Lift whole clumps of shallots together, as they will keep well in their fresh state for a week or so.

Pruning fruit in summer

Where autumn pruning concentrates on the long-term shape and structure of your fruit trees and bushes, the aim of summer pruning is to maintain their immediate size, health, and productivity.

Most pruning tasks now are simple to do, and take just a new minutes, and can make all the difference between having neat, fruitful plants; and a messy garden and a disappointing crop.

Cut down to size

The main focus of summer pruning is to control soft new growth, which not only attracts insect pests, but also restricts airflow at the middle of the plant, encouraging diseases, such as powdery mildew. It is also an opportunity to cut out weak or diseased growth. This is also a good time to train vines.

When pruning, always cut just above an outward-facing bud, using sharp secateurs, cutting at 45° away from the bud. This drains rainwater away from the bud, preventing disease.

RED- AND WHITECURRANTS
Now is the time to prune all of this year's new growth, except the branch leaders, back to five leaves by midsummer. The main formative pruning is done in the winter.

GOOSEBERRIES
To help prevent mildew, prune branches in the middle of the bush to improve air flow. Cut back new growth to five leaves, leaving the leading tips of the branches uncut.

Jo's tips

Gooseberry bushes have a tendency to form droopy branches. To help keep the bush upright, prune to inward- and upward-facing buds, rather than to outward-facing buds, as you normally would with other shrubs and bushes.

Blackcurrants produce their best fruit on last summer's growth, so removing new wood now will affect the following year's crop. Prune these bushes during winter instead.

SUMMER-FRUITING RASPBERRIES
As soon as each cane has finished cropping, untie it from its support and cut it at ground level to remove it completely. Tie the young canes that will fruit next year into the supports.

FAN-TRAINED FIGS
Pinch back the growing tips of new shoots to five leaves. This will encourage lower buds on the shoot to produce embryonic fruit that will overwinter and ripen next summer.

Grape vine pruning

There are two main techniques used to train and prune grapes. The "single cordon" system involves maintaining a single upright stem, from which multiple fruiting laterals are trained against wires. It is often used for indoor grapes.

The "double guyot" system entails training two new branches horizontally each year, from which upright fruiting shoots develop. This system is widely used for outdoor vines. Whichever method you use, summer pruning is essential for a good crop, and to keep your vines under control.

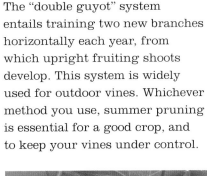

1 TRAIN SINGLE CORDONS
Tie in the central leader against a cane attached to a framework of horizontal wires. Cut back all lateral stems that have no flowers to five leaves from the central leader.

2 CUT BACK LATERALS
On mature plants, cut back flowering lateral stems to two leaves beyond the last truss, and tie them to the wires. Thin surplus trusses and pinch out sideshoots to one leaf.

1 TRAIN DOUBLE GUYOT GRAPES
Tie in new vertical shoots growing from branches trained horizontally in autumn. Remove growing tips at the top wire and any sideshoots. Thin trusses to every 30cm (12in).

2 CHOOSE THREE STEMS
Train three sideshoots upwards from the vine's centre to provide next year's fruiting arms. Tie them into the supporting wires, and pinch back any sideshoots to one leaf as they grow.

PRUNING TOOLS

Choosing the right tool for the job makes pruning easier, and also helps prevent accidental damage, such as tears, occurring to your plants.

Secateurs must be clean and sharp. Use them to cut new growth, and woody material up to pencil thickness.

Pruning saws are ideal for thicker stems and branches, although you need good access to saw effectively.

Loppers can be used to cut stems too thick for secateurs, but too thin for a saw. Avoid twisting them as you cut.

Bow saws are only suitable for cutting thick branches. They are liable to tear smaller stems, causing damage.

PRUNING FRUIT IN SUMMER

August: what to sow

LATE SEASON CROPS

HARVEST: **AUG–DEC**

Make one more sowing of these quick crops now for a last harvest before the end of autumn, although they may need cloching in cooler areas.

ROCKET
Sow in a slightly shaded bed to prevent bolting, 1cm (½in) deep in drill, thinning to 15cm (6in) apart.

KOHL RABI
Ready to crop in 4–5 weeks, sow in 1cm (½in) deep drills, spaced 25cm (10in). Thin to 10cm (4in).

TURNIP
Sow like kohl rabi, and lift some as baby roots in a few weeks, allowing others to mature fully.

SOW

JAPANESE ONIONS

CARROTS

LATE SUMMER VEG

SPRING BULBS

Certain types of onion, often described as Japanese varieties, can be sown towards the end of late summer, and overwintered for an early crop of bulbs in late spring. Try sowing a variety such as 'Buffalo' or 'Senshyu', in rows 30cm (12in) apart and thin to 5–10cm (2–4in) apart. This should give you sturdy young plants that will see out the winter and shoot away quickly in spring.

HARVEST: **MAY–JUN**

LAST CARROTS

To make a last outdoor sowing of carrots, use a faster maturing early-variety, like 'Early Nantes', and cloche the crop at the onset of autumn. Sow thinly in drills with 15cm (6in) between them, and thin seedlings to 5cm (2in) apart. A real advantage of sowing carrots this late is that they shouldn't have any problems with carrot fly.

HARVEST: **AUG–DEC**

August: what to plant

HARDY WINTER CROPS

HARVEST: **VARIOUS**

Spring cauliflowers and winter sprouting broccoli, sown in early summer, will now be ready to transplant into their winter beds. Space them 60cm (2ft) apart each way, firm the soil around plants to stop them rocking in windy weather, and net to keep off hungry pigeons.

'CLARET'
A sprouting broccoli, this is a late maturing variety that crops well into early spring. Good for cooler regions.

'RUDOLPH'
This early sprouting broccoli produces flavour-rich, dark florets in midwinter. Freeze surpluses.

'WINTER AALSMEER'
For well-formed, smaller curds, try this hardy variety. It ripens over a longer period than most hybrids.

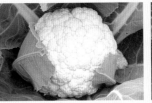

'WALCHEREN WINTER PILGRIM'
Very winter hardy, this robust cauliflower gives a good spring crop of large white heads.

BABY LEAF SALAD

CHICORY

WINTER CAULIFLOWER

PLANT

SALAD LEAVES 24/7

HARVEST: **SEP–FEB**

If you've been sowing salad crops all summer, transplant some seedlings now and bring them under cover for fresh leaves in the lean winter months.

1 PICK YOUR PLANTS
Choose a selection of baby leaf plants, picking the largest, heathiest specimens. Lift them with as much root as possible.

2 POT THEM UP
Fill a large container with compost and plant the baby leaf plants, leaving enough space around each one to grow a little.

3 GROW AND HARVEST
Water well and grow the plants on under cover. Harvest regularly, giving the plants time to re-grow, especially in cold periods.

WINTER CHICORY

Outdoor chicory crops are prone to rotting in wet winter conditions. To enjoy a reliable harvest of leaves during the coldest months, plant module-raised seedlings, sown at the beginning of this month, under cover in a greenhouse or cold frame. Choose red or sugarloaf varieties and plant out them as soon as they're large enough, spacing the plants 20–25cm (8–10in) apart. Water in well.

HARVEST: **OCT–MAR**

August: what to do

LET IN LIGHT
Tomatoes, winter squashes, and pumpkins all need plenty of sunlight to ripen, but the fruit is often shaded by foliage. By late summer, with growth slowing, it's safe to remove some of their overshadowing leaves. Take off the lower leaves of tomato plants so that the more mature fruit trusses near the base ripen first. Any leaves that are shading squashes and pumpkins can be removed.

POTATO BLIGHT
A fungal disease called potato blight commonly occurs in warm, wet summers. The infection causes brown patches on the edges of leaves. Remove affected plant tops as soon as they start to die down. Don't compost them; ideally burn them.

TEND

TOMATOES & SQUASHES

POTATOES

SWEET CORN

RASPBERRIES

READY TO EAT?
Sweet corn tastes good only when perfectly ripe. Wait until the tassels at the top of the cob turn dark brown before checking.

1 CHECK THE COB
Carefully pull back some of the leaves covering a cob. The kernels are ripe when they are a buttery shade of pale yellow.

2 HARVEST LATER
Test several cobs, wrapping each one up again if it is not ripe. It's better to wait until next month than pick too soon.

CUTTING CANES
As soon as the last berry is picked from summer-fruiting raspberries, cut the fruited canes right down to ground level. The new canes that came up this year will be the ones that bear next year's crop. These need to be spread evenly along the supporting wires and tied in with twine. Cut out any new canes that look weak and spindly, leaving only strong, healthy stems coming from each plant.

BEAT THE SLUGS

In some gardens, small soil-dwelling slugs can cause considerable damage by burrowing into potato crops. The spoiled parts can just be cut out if the potatoes are being eaten straight away, but if you plan to store your crop into the winter, slug damage will allow rot to set in. If you see signs of slug attack on crops destined for storage, lift unmarked tubers as soon as possible to minimize the problem. Make sure the potatoes are dry before storing them in paper sacks somewhere cool and dark.

CLEAN UP

Good garden hygiene helps prevent the spread of pests and diseases. When each crop has finished, remove all spent plant material from the bed and compost it, or burn it if disease was present. To help stop diseases building up in the soil, practise crop rotation: grow groups of closely related plants in a different bed each year.

POTATOES

GARDEN HYGIENE

DISEASES

HEALTH CHECK

Hot, dry conditions in summer cause plants stress and leave them vulnerable to disease. Feed and water them, and watch for danger signs.

MAGNESIUM DEFICIENCY
Look out for yellowing leaves. Plants affected include fruit trees, potatoes, and tomatoes. Feed magnesium as a foliar spray.

BROWN ROT
This fungus spreads rapidly among tree fruits, causing rot. Cut off all infected fruits, together with their branch tips, and burn them.

BOTRYTIS (GREY MOULD)
Many plants can be infected by this airborne fungus. Keeping your garden cleared of debris and dead plants is the best defence.

DON'T FORGET

To encourage your cobnuts to produce more fruit buds and to reduce vigour, snap without breaking off lateral shoots over 30cm (12in) long. This practice is called "brutting".

August: what to harvest

SUMMER MELONS

If your melons were sown in April and planted in the greenhouse in May, you'll know when they're ripening because of the rich melon scent that fills the air. Melons are ready to pick when, in addition to their sweet aroma, they're slightly softer at the stalk end, and they come away from the stalk when lifted. Pick when fully ripe and eat immediately. Melons don't store well.

READY OR NOT

It can be tricky to tell when aubergines are ripe because not all varieties develop the tell-tale, smooth, shiny skin. Swelling around the middle of the fruit indicates the seeds are forming, and time to harvest. Cut and cook as soon as possible.

HARVEST

PEPPERS & CHILLIES

MELONS

CELERY

AUBERGINE

PICK YOUR PEPPERS

Both these crops need lots of heat to ripen fully, and during poor summers in cooler regions, even under glass, they may stay green.

1 PICK GREEN
Cut the first full-sized fruits of peppers and chillies while still green, to encourage further fruit to develop on the plants.

2 LEAVE TO RIPEN
Allow later fruit to mature to yellow, orange, or red for a richer, sweeter flavour. Green fruits have a slightly bitter taste.

STEM CELERY

Self-blanching celery will start to become ready over the next few weeks. You can either cut individual stems at the base to use as you need them, or lift the whole plant in one go with a fork. Sown in spring, celery is best eaten as soon as the stems are crisp and juicy. If you can't eat them all, freeze the surplus, or leave plants in the ground until the first frosts. Don't wait too long, as it may become dry and pithy.

LIFT AND DRY BULBS

After a long growing season, spring-sown onions, and garlic planted last autumn are now ready to harvest. Lift garlic bulbs with a fork once their leaves start to yellow, being careful not to bruise the bulbs. The cloves may start to sprout if you leave them too long. Leave onions and shallots until the foliage has died down before gently lifting them. Spread them out on wire mesh or wooden slats outside in the sun to dry for 7–10 days, or do the same in a well-ventilated area indoors if it's wet.

RIPE TO EAT

Now is peak season for cherry, plum, damson, apricot, and peach trees, but exact ripening times depend on variety and weather. Even on a single tree, the fruit will ripen at different times, so check often. To pick, pull plums and damsons from their stalks, cut cherries with their stems, and lift and twist apricots and peaches in your palm.

ONIONS, GARLIC, & SHALLOTS

TREE FRUIT

BLUEBERRIES

BEAUTIFUL BLUEBERRIES

Blueberries, planted in autumn, crop over a few weeks. Pick and eat them as soon as possible. If dry, they will store in the fridge for a few days.

'BLUETTA'
A free-fruiting variety that bears deep blue berries, roughly 1cm (½in) across. It flowers later than many, so is good for cooler regions.

'SPARTAN'
Early-cropping variety with light blue fruit that have a sweet, tangy flavour. Like all blueberries, the taste is more intense when cooked.

'EARLIBLUE'
This variety also crops early, producing a high yield of pale blue fruit, held in conveniently large clusters. Eat fresh or freeze.

HANDY HINT

To help your chillies develop their distinctive fieriness, water them only sparingly as the fruit grows. If you prefer milder chillies, water the plants more.

Saving your own seeds

As well as growing crops to eat, it's easy harvest your own seeds to sow the next year. This not only saves money, it also allows you to select and grow on your favourites, and to produce fresh seed organically. Saving seed also gives you a good excuse to let vegetables bloom, and enjoy flowers you wouldn't normally see.

Saving seed

Collecting home-grown seed is doubly satisfying, as it gives two crops in one. Since you can choose the actual plants you save seed from, you can select those that tasted best or gave the biggest yield. Repeat this process over successive years and you can even develop your own unique strains, just as plant breeders do.

A drawback of saving seeds is that plants must flower, which means leaving them in the ground without harvesting them. This may not be feasible if you have a small crop, or little space to allow the plants to grow on. Also, unless you can isolate the plants, natural cross-pollination between varieties means the seed won't be exactly the same as the parents. This means there's little point saving seed from expensive F1 hybrids, as they won't be true to type.

Jo's tips

Whatever type of seed you save, make sure it is completely dry before storing it in paper bags or small envelopes. Label the packages with the name of the plant and the date the seed was collected. Always store seed in a cool, dry place, protected from mice.

FLOWERS FIRST
To collect seeds, you must first allow the vegetable plants to bloom. Most leaf and root crops are normally harvested before they flower, so to save your own seeds, you need to leave a few plants unharvested.

STORE DRY SEED
Many plants, such as rocket, produce seed in capsules or pods. To harvest these, wait for the pods to turn brown but collect the seeds before they fall to the ground. Empty the seeds out and leave them to dry before storing them.

SEED FROM PODS
Unless the summer is wet, leave fruiting pods, such as beans, on the plants to turn dry and papery. If wet, pick the pods, spread them out to dry indoors, then empty out the seeds.

SEED FROM WET FRUITS
When collecting seeds from moist fruit, such as tomatoes, let the fruit ripen on the plant, pick it, cut it open, and remove the seeds. Spread them on tissue paper to dry, then store.

Salad vegetables such as lettuce run readily to seed. Leave them in the ground and allow them to flower, and collect seeds from the strongest plants.

TRY THESE

The best seeds to collect are those that are expensive to buy, or from crops you plan to grow a lot of next year. You can also share seeds with your friends.

Herbs – Many herbs, such as fennel, caraway, and dill, are grown for their seeds as well as their leaves.

Peas – Leave only the last few pods to mature and dry fully; this will allow the plants to flower and fruit for longer.

Beans – Collect the same way as peas. Dried beans can be used for cooking or sowing. Store them in labelled jars.

Squash and pumpkin – These large fruits are packed with seeds. Collect only those from the best fruits.

September: what to sow

GROW YOUR OWN SOIL IMPROVERS

Sow green manure crops now to protect and improve empty beds during winter. Dig in the young plants 4 weeks before next year's crops are planted, to improve the soil with nutrients and organic matter.

ALFALFA
This plant has a long taproot that penetrates into heavy soil to help break it up and aid drainage.

RED CLOVER
A legume, this plant absorbs nitrogen from the atmosphere and locks it into the soil for plants.

GRAZING RYE
This dense grass helps to suppress weeds, while its fine roots improve soil structure. Good on light soil.

SOW

SPINACH & WINTER LETTUCE

SPRING ONIONS & RADISH

GREEN MANURES

LATE LEAVES

Now is your last chance to sow spinach and winter lettuce to grow on under cover for winter crops. Choose fast-growing spinach varieties, such as 'Triathlon', and winter varieties of butterhead and crisphead lettuce, like 'Valdor' and 'Winter Density'. All will crop through the coldest months. Sow 1cm (½in) deep, and plant out in a cold frame or greenhouse before the end of autumn.

HARVEST: **NOV–MAR**

SOW ONIONS

Make a last sowing of spring onions and radish now. Use a hardy spring onion variety, like 'White Lisbon', for a winter crop, sowing thinly, 1cm (½in) deep, in rows 15cm (6in) apart. In cold areas, cloche spring onions in winter. Also sow summer radishes thinly in drills 1cm (½in) deep, thinning to 2cm (¾in), to crop in autumn.

HARVEST: **OCT–DEC**

September: what to plant

FEELING PEACHY

HARVEST: **AUG–SEPT**

Container-grown trees can be planted at any time, but wait until winter to plant bare-root specimens. Dig in plenty of compost, especially at the base of walls, and plant to the same depth as the soil mark on the trunk. Water well and stake, or fix fan-trained trees with wires.

PEACH 'DUKE OF YORK'
Grown against a warm wall, this variety will produce a good crop of large, yellow-fleshed fruit.

PEACH 'PEREGRINE'
This is a heavy-cropping variety, with sweet, red-flushed fruit. Give it a warm, sunny, sheltered site.

NECTARINE 'FANTASIA'
This hardy variety produces large, juicy, yellow-fleshed fruit that ripen throughout July. Suitable for pots.

NECTARINE 'LORD NAPIER'
Late-ripening, this variety has thin-skinned, very juicy fruit that mature red. A reliable cropper.

JAPANESE ONIONS

SPRING CABBAGE

PEACHES & NECTARINES

PLANT

ONION SETS

HARVEST: **MAY–JUN**

For the earliest onions to harvest next year, plant out sets of Japanese over-wintering varieties, such as 'Buffalo', outdoors.

1 PLANT THE SETS
In a sunny, weed-free bed, push each set into the soil so that just the lip is showing.

2 FIRM THEM IN
Space the sets 5–10cm (2–4in) apart, and allow about 30cm (12in) between rows.

PLANT OUT CABBAGES

Between now and mid-autumn, transplant spring cabbages, sown in modules or seedbeds, into their final positions for overwintering. Find a sunny spot, with fertile soil that has not recently been dug over or manured. This will avoid the plants producing soft leafy growth that can be damaged by frosts. Space plants 30cm (12in) apart each way to encourage good-sized heads.

HARVEST: **APR–JUN**

September: what to do

CUT DOWN ASPARAGUS
The tall feathery fronds of asparagus will have turned yellow now and may be starting to topple over. Cut them down with a pair of sharp secateurs, clipping off the stems as close to the soil as possible. The foliage is prickly, so be careful how you handle it. Once you have cleared the asparagus bed, spread a well-rotted organic mulch over it to help keep the soil in good condition for next year.

FEED LEEKS
A bed of large, healthy leeks should see you through winter. These tough plants rarely require watering, but they do benefit from an occasional feed with a balanced liquid fertilizer, so give them a boost before the end of the growing season.

TEND

PROTECT

ASPARAGUS

CELERIAC

LEEKS

FROST PROTECTION
Early autumn is often mild, but if you live in a cool area where night frosts are likely, then consider covering your late crops.

FLEECE TUNNEL
Make a protective tunnel cloche by securing horticultural fleece over wire hoops. You can easily remove the fleece in the daytime.

PVC CLOCHE
This type of cloche can be left open during the day for ventilation. For frost protection, close off the ends at night with plastic sheeting.

CELERIAC CARE
To encourage the stems of celeriac to bulk out for a good winter crop, regularly remove any damaged or older leaves. Just pull them away with a firm tug near the base of the plant. The tops of the swollen stems will soon start to appear above the soil. Celeriac plants will benefit from plenty of water during dry weather. The regular application of a balanced liquid fertilizer will also help to keep them growing strongly.

EMPTY THE BINS

Autumn may see a glut of compostable waste as plants die back and you tidy up for the winter. Make room for this by using up what is already in your compost bin. Apply a mulch of home-produced compost around crops that are going to overwinter or add it to recently cleared beds. With your bin empty, you can start again. Plants that have finished cropping mix well with autumn garden prunings, grass clippings, and fallen leaves to produce more compost for the following year.

RIPEN INDOORS

If frost threatens, take action to salvage the remainder of your outdoor tomatoes. Cut down cordon varieties, and either hang them up or lay them out flat, somewhere light to let the fruit finish ripening, in either a greenhouse, garage, or conservatory. Container-grown bush varieties can simply be moved under cover and grown on.

COMPOST

TOMATOES

PERENNIAL HERBS

LIFT AND DIVIDE HERBS

This is the ideal time to lift and divide perennial herbs, such as mint, either to plant in the garden or to pot-up and bring them indoors for a winter crop.

1 LIFT THE PLANT
Large clumps of herbs need splitting. Use a fork or spade to lift the entire plant from the soil. Tip out established pot-grown plants.

2 SPLIT OFF CLUMPS
For larger divisions, use your hands or a hand fork to break off clumps from the original rootball, which you can then replant.

3 TAKE CUTTINGS
Propagate from the spreading stems, or runners, of mint by taking cuttings of small rooted sections and potting up.

DON'T FORGET

As you do your autumn tidying, clear up as you go along. Don't leave piles of clippings and other debris lying around to rot and harbour pests. Compost or burn them as soon as possible.

September: what to harvest

PICK APPLES AND PEARS NOW

As the main season for harvesting apples and pears begins, it's now time to start checking the fruit on your trees for ripeness. To do this, lift apples gently in your hand, and if they come away easily with their stalk intact, they're ready to eat. Pears are trickier. Early-autumn ripening varieties should be picked when slightly underripe or they will become brown-centred and mealy. Test pears regularly, and if they come away with a lift and a gentle twist, then pick them and leave in a cool place for several days to ripen fully.

CUT CABBAGE, LIFT LEEKS

Red and summer cabbages, sown in March and planted out in May, can be cut as soon as the heads are a usable size. They should crop well into autumn, but they won't survive very cold weather. Once mature, some varieties stand in the ground longer than others, but watch out for signs of bolting, which spoils them. The first leeks, sown in spring, are ready for lifting. Harvest later-sown crops through winter into spring.

HARVEST

RASPBERRIES   APPLES & PEARS   CABBAGE & LEEKS

AUTUMN TREATS

Autumn raspberries, planted in October, bear ample fruit from now until the first frosts. Less favoured by birds than earlier varieties, they shouldn't require netting, although the tough cores mean they're more fiddly to prepare. They are best eaten as fresh.

'AUTUMN BLISS'
This variety is shorter than most and can be grown without support. It fruits freely, producing tasty red-pink berries, well into autumn.

'JOAN J'
Spine-free and self-supporting, this compact, sweet-tasting variety is suitable for containers. Keep it well watered and fed if pot grown.

'POLKA'
This variety bears especially large fruit that are produced in abundance until November. The berries are noted for their taste and sweetness.

'ALL GOLD'
Similar to 'Autumn Bliss', it's fruit matures yellow and doesn't stain clothes or fingers, so is ideal for gardeners with young children.

GOLDEN SWEET CORN

Sweet corn tells you it's ready to pick when the silk tassels at the top of the cobs turn brown. To be completely sure it's ripe, pull back the leaves that surround the cob and look for pale, butter-yellow kernels. Sweet corn sown inside in April, and planted in June, should be ready now. To pick it, twist the cobs from the stems, snapping them at the base. Their sweetness rapidly fades, so use them quickly, otherwise blanch and freeze them. Sweet corn doesn't keep well in the fridge.

LIFT POTATOES

Cut potato plants off to just above ground level in early autumn, leaving the tubers in the soil to mature for 2 weeks before lifting with a fork. Lift those for storage on a dry, sunny day, and leave them on the soil surface for up to 2 hours to dry without going green. Store undamaged tubers in large paper sacks, in a dark, frost-free place.

SQUASH & PUMPKINS

SWEET CORN

FIGS

POTATOES

BUMPER CROPS

Squashes and pumpkins sown in April should be cut fresh when required. To store, pick mature fruit with plenty of stem, when they're well coloured and the stem has cracked. Before the frosts come, cure the fruit for 10 days in the sun outdoors, or in a greenhouse or indoors in poor weather, to harden the skin so that they keep. Store in a cool, frost-free place.

SWEET FIGS

Figs don't ripen further once picked, so wait until they're hanging heavy from the tree and feel soft. If sap appears at the base of the fruit, it's a good indication of ripeness. Pick the fruit carefully without bruising it and eat quickly. Figs keep fresh for a week or so in a cool place, but are also excellent cooked.

Getting ready for winter

Winter still seems a long way off but around now, nights turn cooler and the days shorten, signalling the timely end of summer and that it's time to get ready for the season to come. With so much to harvest right now, it's hard to think ahead, but take advantage of September's golden weather to get a few jobs done.

Healthy balance

Tidying up your growing spaces is important to help prevent pests and diseases from lingering in plant waste, ready to attack new growth in spring, and to stop mats of fallen leaves from smothering over-wintering plants, such as perennial herbs. Weeds will still be growing now, so don't allow them to take hold at this late stage, either.

However, it's important to strike a balance. Wildlife relies on food and shelter to survive the cold winter months in the garden. A pile of leaves left in a corner or under a hedge, or a small log pile, is enough to make a winter home for hedgehogs and beneficial insects. Birds will flock to fallen fruit during a cold snap, and to any plants you allow to run to seed. Leave your plot tidy, but not bare during winter.

Jo's tips

If you have large trees in or near your garden, and you have the space, construct a post and chicken wire cage for making leaf mould. Tree leaves compost more slowly than many other types of garden waste, so it's a good idea to keep them out of the usual heap.

MULCH BARE SOIL
Bare soil and winter weather are not a good combination. Heavy rain leaches nutrients from the soil and ruins its structure. Apply thick mulch to large gaps between plants, and to beds after you have removed spent crops.

GENERAL TIDY UP
Clear away weeds, finished crops, and general plant debris from your beds and containers to prevent pests and diseases overwintering among them. Also rake up fallen leaves to stop them smothering your winter crops.

FIT GREASE BANDS
To help protect your fruit trees from insect damage, tie grease bands to the trunks, 60cm (2ft) above the ground. This will trap pests making their way the trunk to lay their eggs.

SUNDRY ROUND UP
Round up pots, labels, wire, watering cans, and other odds and ends that have become scattered during the growing season. Clean and dry them before storing them tidily.

CLEAN UP

Many essential autumn tasks are quick to do but are easily forgotten. Tidy your shed and clean your equipment to keep it in good working condition.

Clean secateurs using wire wool to remove sticky sap and other debris that has adhered to the blades.

Wipe off canes and plant supports used during summer. Tie them in bundles and store under cover.

Before the first hard frost, check you have enough fleece to protect crops and insulation for your greenhouse.

Remove greenhouse shading now – any remaining crops will need all the heat they can get from the sun.

Collect fallen leaves periodically to make leaf mould (see Jo's Tips, opposite) before they pile up, smothering over-wintering crops, and harbouring pests and diseases.

October: what to sow

SOW CAULIFLOWER

For an extra early crop of summer cauliflowers, sow them now under cover into modules or drills 1cm (½in) deep. Thin drill-sown seedlings as they grow to 10cm (4in) apart, ready for transplanting in spring. Keep the seedlings protected but not heated until then. Water as required, and protect them against slugs.

HARVEST: **MAY–JUN**

EXTRA EARLY BEANS

HARVEST: **APR–JUN**

If you have a well-drained soil, and want extra-early broad beans, sow hardy varieties now, 5cm (2in) deep, and protect the plants with cloches.

'STEREO'
This variety is like mangetout in that you can eat the entire pods. They can also be eaten skinned.

'SUPER AQUADULCE'
This is one of the hardiest bean varieties, and is suitable for growing in colder areas.

'THE SUTTON'
A dwarf variety, suitable for smaller gardens, it produces large pods with five beans apiece.

SOW

GARLIC

SUMMER CAULIFLOWER

PEAS

BROAD BEANS

GROW GARLIC

HARVEST: **JUN–AUG**

Garlic needs a long growing season, and on well-drained soil it can be planted outside now. If you have a heavy soil, plant in small pots under cover for now.

1 BREAK UP BULB
Buy certified disease-free garlic bulbs and break them into individual cloves, removing most of the outer papery layers of the bulb.

2 PREPARE SITE
Choose fertile soil that has not been recently manured, dig it over lightly, and rake it to remove any large clods and stones.

3 PLANT OUT
Push cloves into the soil, 2cm (¾in) deep, 20cm (8in) apart each way. Plant flat-end down. Use a dibber to make holes if it helps.

SUPER EARLY PEAS

Even tough pea seeds will rot in wet winter soils, but if yours is well-drained, or you have a raised bed that drains freely, you can sow now for an extra early crop. Choose early varieties, like 'Feltham First', and sow thinly, 4cm (1½in) deep in drills, about 15cm (6in) wide. Insert pea sticks or taut plastic netting for support, and tie in the young plants as they grow. Cover plants in extreme weather.

HARVEST: **MAY–JUN**

October: what to plant

BLACKBERRIES, RASPBERRIES, & FAMILY

HARVEST: **JUL–OCT**

Bare-rooted blackberries, raspberries, and their hybrids (below), should be planted now. Plant raspberries 45cm (18in) apart, 8–10cm (3–4in) deep, with 1.5m (5ft) between rows. Plant blackberries and hybrids 2m (6ft) apart. Cut canes to a bud 25cm (10in) above the soil.

BOYSENBERRY
A cross between a blackberry, loganberry, and raspberry, its dark red fruit have a rich bramble taste.

LOGANBERRY
Best grown like a blackberry, the fruit tastes like a sharp raspberry, and is best cooked with lots of sugar.

TAYBERRY
Ripening dark red, this vigorous hybrid produces sweet-tasting fruit over a very long period.

JAPANESE WINEBERRY
This distinct species has small, soft, orange-red berries with an unusual wine-like flavour.

SUMMER BERRIES

PLANT

GOOSEBERRIES & CURRANTS

WITLOOF CHICORY

PLANT BARE ROOTED
Plant bare-root gooseberries and currants now in a sunny, sheltered site, in fertile, well-drained soil. Soak first, setting gooseberries, red- and whitecurrants 1.5m (5ft) apart, and blackcurrants 1.8m (6ft) apart. Plant to the same depth as the soil mark on the stems, then prune. Choose blackcurrant plants that are certified free of blackcurrant reversion virus.

HARVEST: **VARIOUS**

FORCED CHICORY
If you want Witloof chicory roots to force indoors for winter, lift plants sown in May, from now until early winter. Leave the roots in a shed for a week, cut off all the leaves 2cm (¾in) above the root, and store them flat in sand-filled boxes. These can then be potted up in December, ready for forcing for a New Year crop.

HARVEST: **JAN–MAR**

October: what to do

STORE IN THE SOIL

As the foliage on tall Jerusalem artichoke stems dies back, its goodness is taken up by the underground tubers. Once the leaves are brown, cut the stems down to 8–10cm (3–4in) above the soil, and chop them into small pieces for composting. Leave the tubers where they are, because they keep best in the soil.

GREENHOUSEKEEPING

Keep your greenhouse free from pests and diseases and insulated from the winter cold. Mid-autumn is a good time for these maintenance jobs.

1 CLEAN
Clear plant debris, wipe away shading paint with a dry cloth, and clean the glass inside and out.

2 DISINFECT
Scrub glazing bars, hard paths, and shelves or staging with a diluted disinfectant solution.

3 INSULATE
Cut sheets of bubble wrap to fit the framework of the glazing. Do not block the vents.

TEND

ARTICHOKES

CELERIAC

CONTAINER-GROWN FRUIT

GREENHOUSES

WARM BEDDING

With the right preparation, both parsnips and celeriac can be left in the soil during the winter. To protect their roots from extremely cold weather, or to prevent soil freezing and enable lifting during winter, mulch them with a thick layer of straw. Celeriac keeps its leaves throughout the winter, so tuck the straw under the leaves to make sure that the roots have maximum protection from frosts.

REPOT FRUIT

For good yields you must repot fruit trees and bushes every year until they are full sized. Knock the plant out of its pot in mid- to late autumn and tease the roots out of the edge of the rootball. Repot into a container about 10cm (4in) wider at the top than the last. Use John Innes No. 2 compost for soft fruit and John Innes No. 3 for trees.

PROTECT SALAD CROPS

Many leafy vegetable crops, such as winter lettuce, chard, and spinach, are resistant to cold and can be kept going well into the winter. However, they need some protection because their foliage can quickly be ruined by harsh and wet weather. Cloching your crops at this stage in the season will protect the plants from the worst of the weather, allowing them to keep producing fresh leaves for longer. If you take precautions now, you will have top-quality leaves available for picking into winter.

BRING INDOORS

Citrus trees in containers that have enjoyed a sheltered, sunny spot outside all summer should now be brought back indoors. Find them a well-ventilated place, with plenty of light and a minimum temperature of 7°C (45°F). Keep them away from radiators and cold draughts. They will not need further feeding until spring.

SALAD CROPS

CITRUS

ROOT CROPS

LIFTING AND STORING ROOTS

Root crops, such as Jerusalem artichoke, can be left in the ground during winter and actually store better in the soil. However, if your soil is heavy or you live in a cold area, it's worth being cautious and lifting what you can now to store under cover.

CARROTS
Dig up before the frosts and cut off the foliage to within 1cm (½in) of the root. Store in layers in soil or sand-filled boxes. Keep frost free.

POTATOES
Lift potatoes on a dry day and leave them on the soil surface to dry for a few hours. Store in paper sacks or in a clamp if you have a large crop.

BEETROOT
As with carrots, lift the roots before the first frost, and snap off the leaves. Store in layers in sand-filled boxes kept somewhere frost free.

TURNIPS
These can be harvested until winter, but if the weather allows, lift them now and store the roots in boxes of dry soil or sand. Keep frost free.

October: what to harvest

LAST SUMMER HARVEST
For a final taste of fresh summer vegetables, go out picking now while the weather allows, and harvest the last of your peas, sweetcorn, marrows, courgettes, carrots, cucumbers, and Florence fennel, before they're spoiled by the frost. Many of these plants will already be winding down for winter, so harvest and enjoy what is there, then remove and compost any remaining plant material.

CELERY STICKS
Don't delay in lifting the last of your self-blanching celery, sown in February, because it won't survive in the soil through frost. Stems deteriorate in quality anyway through autumn. The small, inner stems keep well if stored in a plastic bag in a cool place after harvest.

HARVEST

LATE SUMMER CROPS

CELERY

NUTS

APPLES & PEARS

HARVEST NUTS NOW
Nuts are a real mid-autumn treat that should not be overlooked. Pick cobnuts from among the branches when their shells have hardened and turned brown. If you're lucky enough to have a walnut tree, gather the nuts from the ground as soon as they have fallen, remove their husks straight away, and scrub the shells to remove husk fibres before drying. Both types of nut can be eaten fresh now, or spread out in a warm place and allowed to dry for storage in a cool, airy place. They will keep well for weeks; check occasionally for pest damage.

LATE APPLES AND PEARS
Late varieties of apples and pears should be left on the tree to ripen for as long as possible. Even then, most pears will stay hard and need a period of storage to bring them to perfection. The trick is to leave the fruit on the tree for as long as you can, hoping that it won't be knocked off and damaged by autumn weather, making it useless for storing. Of course, any windfall apples and pears will still be delicious, although they cannot be stored because of their impact bruises. If you have a glut, juice them or make them into wine.

PICK YOUR OWN GRAPES

Grapes require patience, because even though they may look ripe, they need time on the vine to allow the fruit sugars to develop.

Mid-autumn grapes need 4 weeks, late varieties want 10 weeks. When picking, use secateurs to avoid spoiling the fruits' white bloom.

'BOSKOOP GLORY'
This is a good dessert variety for cooler areas, and gives a reliable harvest of delicious dark grapes that can be eaten straight from the vine.

'REGENT'
A vigorous variety, it bears large, sweet blue-black fruit. Its foliage also develops rich colouring, so it doubles as an ornamental climber.

'SIEGERREBE'
Dessert grape, its sweet, juicy fruit ripen with a rich brown tint, and can be eaten fresh or used to make wine. It is suitable for cooler regions.

'MÜLLER-THURGAU'
This variety is widely grown for wine-making, and is a good choice for cooler areas. The grapes are also sweet enough to eat fresh.

BEANS

GRAPES

TOMATOES, PEPPERS, & CHILLIES

LAST BEANS
Now brings the last crops of French and runner beans that have been growing all summer. Pick bright and tender pods whole. If your French bean pods are swollen and stringy, leave them to mature, then bring them indoors to dry fully. The white beans inside are actually haricot beans, and can be stored dry. Runner beans are not as palatable dried in this way.

RIPEN INDOORS
If your last harvested tomatoes are refusing to ripen, put them in a paper bag or fruit bowl with some bananas, which give off natural fruit-ripening vapours. Peppers and chillies won't ripen further once picked. Green peppers don't keep well, but freeze your chillies whole and use them when needed.

Starting a compost heap

Every garden, however small, should have at least one compost heap to provide free and fabulous soil improver. The process could not be simpler – in goes green and twiggy garden debris, and kitchen peelings that would otherwise go in the waste bin, and in 6–12 months, out comes amazing, crumbly garden compost.

Making compost

To make good compost, mix waste material together as you build the heap, to allow moisture and air to penetrate into the centre. This creates ideal conditions for the correct bacteria, fungi, and insects to flourish, and quickly break down the waste, without any nasty smells. A good mix of about half carbon-rich woody material and half nitrogen-rich green material helps to keep composting organisms working well.

Check your heap regularly, and if it is wet and slimy and smells bad, then too much nitrogen-rich waste, such as vegetable peelings, has been added. To remedy this, mix in small or shredded woody material. Similarly, a dry heap won't break down quickly, so mix in moist green waste, add water, and turn the heap if the edges dry out.

MIX IT UP
Avoid adding material in thick layers, which will prevent air and moisture circulating. When adding lots of one type, mix it into the heap using a fork.

To achieve finished compost, stop adding fresh waste material when your bin is full, and cover the top with old carpet or the lid. Wait for the level in the bin to stop going down and turn the contents to

TURN REGULARLY
You need to turn your heap at least once to make good compost. The easiest way is to have another, empty heap, and swap material across.

make sure all material is fully broken down. The compost should then be ready in a month or two, so have a second bin to fill in the meantime. Once the first bin is finished, empty it and start again.

Types of compost bins

Choose to make or buy a bin that suits your garden. Site it in sun or part shade, directly on the soil, rather than on paving, to help attract beneficial organisms. Work out how much waste you will have to put on the heap, and try to match this to the size of your bin. Also consider access, and pick a design you can reach into easily when filling or emptying the bin.

(left to right) **Build your own bin** to look attractive or blend into the background, with sliding slats at the front for hassle-free turning. **Plastic bins** are compact and cheap, and offer a quick way to get started, but aren't always easy to turn. **Builder's bags** are large and often free, and are a good option for allotments or large gardens.

TRY THESE

Compost heaps need a mixture of moist and dry material. Avoid adding in perennial weeds, cooked food, diseased growth, and thick branches.

Vegetable peelings contain nitrogen and moisture; collect them along with tea bags and coffee grounds.

Shredded paper and card are great for adding carbon to wet, nitrogen-rich compost. Avoid plastic-coated paper.

Prunings and annual weeds make up the bulk of a compost heap. Avoid composting any diseased material.

Thin woody prunings, less than a pencil thickness, help to aerate larger compost heaps, and also add bulk.

Compost heaps can be just that, a straightforward heap. If you have space, and somewhere to keep it out of sight, simply pile up your garden waste into a heap and it will slowly compost.

STARTING A COMPOST HEAP

November: what to plant

THRIVING VINES

Vines thrive in sunshine and a well-drained, enriched soil. Before planting, put up horizontal wires, spaced 30cm (12in) apart. Plant the vines 1.2–1.5m (4–5ft) apart. Between now and early spring, prune the stems down to two buds above the soil or graft union.

HARVEST: **AUG–NOV**

TIME FOR TREES

Plant fruit trees while the soil is warm and the plants are dormant. Choose a well-drained, sunny site away from frost pockets. Allow each tree ample space, dig in compost, and drive in a stake for free-standing trees or put up horizontal wires for wall-trained trees. Dig a hole, spread out the roots, backfill and firm the soil gently. Keep the trunk 5cm (2in) from the stake.

HARVEST: **VARIOUS**

PLANT

BLUEBERRIES

RHUBARB

GRAPE VINES

FRUIT TREES

POT BLUEBERRIES

Blueberries are easy to grow if you can get the soil right. They need a moist, acid soil with a pH of 4–5.5, so unless your garden naturally has these conditions grow them in pots filled with ericaceous compost. Knock plants from their pots and plant 1.5m (5ft) apart in the soil, or in containers a little larger than their rootball. Firm the soil lightly and water thoroughly. Keep moist until established.

HARVEST: **AUG–SEPT**

RHUBARB SETS

Well-fed rhubarb plants will crop prolifically for many years. Choose an unshaded patch and improve the soil with a generous amount of well-rotted manure before planting. Space the sets (young plants) at least 90cm (36in) apart and plant them with their crowns just above soil level to stop rot setting into the new buds during winter.

HARVEST: **MAR–JUL**

HARDY HERBS

HARVEST: **VARIOUS**

Many tough perennial herbs, such as mint and fennel, are happy to be planted out in late autumn. Unless they are in a sheltered position, Mediterranean herbs, such sage, thyme, and rosemary, may struggle through cold winters when newly planted. Protect them with fleece.

BAY
This tolerant shrubby herb will grow in full sun or partial shade, in moist or dry soil. It is best in milder areas.

CHIVES
Plant this bulb-forming herb in full sun and well-drained soil. It will tolerate shade but becomes leggy.

LEMON BALM
This is a hardy, highly aromatic herb that grows best in a sunny site with free-draining soil. Good in pots.

ROSEMARY
Grow this woody herb in a sheltered, sunny site, with well-drained soil. It is best in milder regions.

FIGS

PATIO FRUIT

PERENNIAL HERBS

MAKE A FIG PIT

HARVEST: **AUG–SEP**

Figs are vigorous plants that are often planted in a restricted area to stop them growing too large.

1 DIG THE PIT
Dig a hole 60cm (24in) square and deep. Line the sides with paving slabs and put in a layer of rubble, allowing good drainage.

2 PLANT AND SUPPORT
Fill the hole with good topsoil, attach strong horizontal supporting wires to the wall, 30cm (12in) apart, then plant and tie in the fig.

FRUIT IN POTS

The full range of fruit trees will flourish in containers, which restrict the size that trees can grow to. This is the ideal way to grow fruit in small gardens. Choose a pot a little bigger than the root system and layer the base with crocks. Plant the tree in the soil at the same level as the original soil mark on the stem. Back fill firmly with John Innes No. 3 compost. Water in well and keep the tree moist.

HARVEST: **VARIOUS**

November: what to do

MARK PARSNIPS
These hardy roots will happily sit in the soil over winter, so if you are short of storage space, they can stay in the ground until you need them. But finding them once their leaves have died down, or if there is snow on the ground, can involve a bit of guesswork. Take a moment to mark the rows with canes that are easy to spot, to make it easier to earth up your parsnip crop later on.

WORK SOIL
Late autumn is the ideal time to cultivate heavy, clay soils, working in organic matter to improve the structure. Digging sticky soils is hard work but allows frosts to help break the clods into crumbs by repeated freezing and thawing. Light, sandy soils are best protected with mulch now and dug over in early spring.

TEND

PARSNIPS

DIG BEDS

WINTER POTS

PREPARING POTS FOR WINTER
Planted or empty, pots and pot-grown plants can be damaged in winter, particularly by frosts (above). Take time now to protect them.

Smaller pots, and those made from terracotta and thin materials are most at risk. Heavy concrete pots are usually winter-proof.

CLEAN EMPTY POTS
Pots made of porous materials may become stained by algae or lime scale. Although harmless, take the opportunity to clean your pots now.

LINE CLAY POTS
In colder areas, line pots with bubble plastic before planting trees in them, to help protect the roots from hard frosts. Don't block drainage holes.

RAISE POTS OFF GROUND
To help keep terracotta pots dry in winter, and protect them against frost damage, raise them off the ground to ensure they drain freely.

WRAP TENDER POTS
In colder areas, protect your pots, and any plant roots inside, from hard frost by wrapping them in bubble plastic, fleece, or hessian sacking.

PROTECT TALL POTS

Safeguard larger container-grown plants, such as fruit trees and bushes, and shrubby herbs, from winter damage, by moving them to a sheltered spot. Strong winds can blow plants over and break containers. Pot-grown plants are also at risk of frosted roots, so move tender plants nearer to the house for warmth.

PRUNE OUTDOOR VINES

Now is the time to prune outdoor vines trained using the double guyot system, where two arms are tied horizontally to bear vertical, fruiting shoots.

1 REMOVE SPENT STEMS
Using sharp secateurs or loppers, cut out the two horizontal arms that fruited last summer. Cut them close to the main stem.

2 PLAN AHEAD
Cut back the middle shoot to three healthy buds. This will grow and bear the three new shoots to train the following season.

3 TRAIN NEW SHOOTS
Tie down the two outer shoots, trained in summer, onto the wire; one to the left, one to the right. These will sprout fruiting stems.

TALL POT PLANTS

WINTER PROTECTION

GRAPES

FALLEN LEAVES

COLD COMFORT

Most crops that grow through winter are fully hardy but can still be damaged by harsh winter winds and rain. If you live in an exposed area, it's well worth providing extra support for taller crops, such as Brussels sprouts and kale, by staking them. Short wooden stakes are best, hammered in close to each plant. If you have a small bed of crops, consider screening right around it with windbreak fabric.

LEAF MOULD

Rather than burning fallen leaves, pile them into their own composting bay to slowly break down into leaf mould. Construct a simple bin using posts and wire mesh, fill with leaves, and in a year or two you'll have crumbly compost for potting and mulching. If space is limited, and you have few leaves, compost them in damp plastic bags.

November: what to harvest

ROOT THEM OUT

Having grown all summer, Jerusalem artichokes have now died back until spring, so you can start lifting the strange-looking, knobbly tubers, with their delicious, nutty flavour. Dig them out using a fork only when needed in the kitchen, as they soon dry out and spoil. The roots keep very well in the soil and can be dug up all through winter, providing the ground isn't frozen. When lifting the tubers, be sure to get even the tiniest ones, because they will re-grow and spread next year if left behind. This perennial crop can be invasive.

FROSTED FIRST

From a spring sowing, parsnips can be lifted now, although they develop the sweetest flavour after a few frosts, so leave some to lift through winter. In light soils the roots can reach a good length. Loosen the earth around them with a fork, and lift them carefully to avoid damage. They're best harvested as required because they keep better in the ground.

HARVEST

JERUSALEM ARTICHOKES

PARSNIPS

KOHL RABI

KOHL SHORTAGE

Late-growing kohl rabi plants endure cold weather, but will be spoiled by frost. Either pull them up and use the swollen stems before winter arrives, cloche the remaining plants, or lift them, remove the outer leaves and store in boxes of sand in a cool, frost-free place.

'PURPLE DANUBE'
Dark on the outside, its tasty flesh is pure white, and most tender when harvested young. Older, larger plants can become slightly bitter tasting.

'KOLIBRI'
Best eaten golf-ball sized, and ready in as little as 8 weeks, this variety is good in smaller gardens where it will give several crops during summer.

'LANRO'
Harvest when the swollen green stems reach 5cm (2in) across. They can be eaten diced and boiled, but are delicious grated in salads.

'SUPERSCHMELZ'
Gradually reaching 25cm (10in) across, this is a larger variety that can also be harvested small. It has a mild, sweet, turnip-like flavour.

HARVEST SALSIFY ROOTS

Salsify, sown directly outside in May, is ready to harvest, allowing you the chance to enjoy the unusual, nutty-tasting roots that have become a 'must have' among top chefs. Dig deeply with a fork to lift the roots as required, from now until spring. Roots left in the soil have a superior flavour to those lifted and stored in sand-filled boxes, but storing is useful in areas with cold winters, where the ground may freeze. The skins must be removed; smaller roots are easier to peel after cooking.

SWEDE SUCCESS

Hearty swedes, sown in May, will be full of flavour. Harvest them as needed until midwinter. If the weather allows, dig them up and store them in dry boxes, covered with sand. If the weather is poor, wait until spring, although the roots will be woody and tougher to eat by then.

SALSIFY

WINTER SALAD

SWEDE

CELERIAC

WINTER CELERIAC

Celeriac can be harvested this month, right through until spring, making it a really useful crop. The roots are tough enough to be left in the ground all winter in most places, and lifted as required. If you live in a very cold area, where the ground may freeze, lift the entire crop now, trim off the outer leaves, and store the roots in boxes of dry sand.

TAKE A LEAF

Winter salad leaves, grown under cover since late summer, are ready to crop. Mizuna, mibuna, oriental mustard, salad rocket, lettuce, perpetual spinach, and corn salad are all plants to take baby leaves from throughout winter. Even under cover, growth will be slow at this time, so these cut-and-come-again crops will take time to re-sprout.

Choosing and planting fruit trees

Fruit trees will be with you for years to come, so consider your choices carefully, and if planting more than one, select early, mid- and late varieties for a longer harvest. Some fruit trees need a pollinator to grow alongside, while others are self-fertile and can be planted singly. Many trees are also grafted to control their size. Seek advice from a fruit nursery to help decide what best suits you and your plot.

Choosing a tree

Once you have decided which fruit to grow there are still other considerations, too. For instance, would you prefer sweet dessert fruit or a culinary variety suited to cooking and preserving?

Fruit trees are grafted onto a rootstock, which determines their final size. Dwarfing rootstocks are ideal for smaller gardens, but need good soil to thrive, whereas semi-dwarfing rootstocks tolerate a wider range of conditions.

Many trees need a partner with an overlapping flowering period for pollination to occur and fruit to set. Varieties that flower at the same time are classed in the same pollination group, and for a good crop, plant two from the same group. If you lack space for two trees, look for possible pollinators growing in neighbouring plots.

Planting in pots

Growing fruit trees in pots limits their size, which is ideal for smaller plots. Select a container 8cm (3in) wider than the root system, ensure it has drainage holes, and add crocks to improve drainage further. Using soil-based compost, fill around the roots to the soil mark on the stem. Stake, firm in, and water the new tree well.

CONTAINER GROWN
Container-grown trees are available year-round. They can be planted at any time of year, but preferably not during hot summer weather. They can be expensive to buy.

BARE-ROOT
Field-grown, bare-root trees are lifted and sold dormant, mainly by specialist nurseries, in autumn and winter. Plant immediately, soaking the roots. Only buy well-rooted, undamaged plants.

PLANTING IN POTS
The best fruit trees to grow in containers are compact varieties grafted onto semi-dwarfing rootstocks. Ask your fruit supplier to recommend suitable varieties.

Planting new trees

The basic approach to planting container-grown and bare-root trees is similar, although there are important differences.

When planting container-grown trees, tease some of the outer roots away from the rootball first, to help them establish properly in the surrounding soil. A good bare-root tree has plenty of spreading roots, which should be soaked before planting if they look dry. Trim any that are damaged.

Always stake new trees to steady them in the wind, and to allow new roots to establish into the soil without being broken.

1 DIG A HOLE
Choose a sunny site, sheltered from wind and any frost pockets. Dig a hole large enough for the roots. If planting bare-root trees, mound the soil in the centre. Hammer in a stake.

2 POSITION THE TREE
Place the tree in the hole, level with the soil mark on the stem. Spread out the roots and ease soil around them, firming well. Attach the tree to the stake using a cushioned tie.

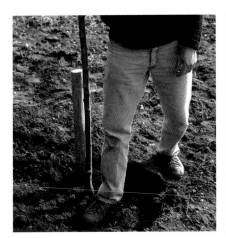

3 WATER AND FIRM IN WELL
Firm the tree in, ensuring the trunk is upright. Water it in well and apply a thick mulch of organic matter to help conserve moisture and gradually nourish the establishing tree.

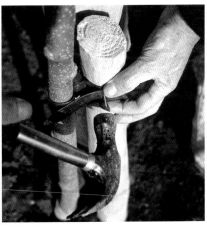

4 STAKING AND AFTERCARE
Attach the tree tie to the stake using a nail. Check a few weeks later to ensure the tie is still in place, and is not rubbing against the tree. Adjust if necessary. Keep the tree watered.

Trained trees

Espaliers and cordons take up little space trained against a wall or fence, making them ideal for smaller gardens. Cordons are single stems, usually trained at a 45° angle, with lots of short, fruiting sideshoots; while espaliers have long arms branching from a central stem, so need more room. These tree forms are controlled by summer pruning. Buy ready-trained trees from specialist nurseries to avoid much of the formative, autumn pruning of young trees.

Espalier – The orderly tiers of a well-trained espalier look magnificent, but need plenty of space to spread; allow 3m (10ft) for trees grafted on dwarfing rootstocks. Espalier trees are usually limited to two or three tiers.

Cordons – This single-stemmed form suits apples and pears. It requires only 75cm (30in) between each tree, which means several varieties can be trained along an average-sized garden fence. Avoid tip-bearing varieties, which won't fruit well when pruned in this way.

December: what to sow

FORCING CHICORY

HARVEST: **JAN–MAR**

Having lifted and stored your Witloof chicory roots, they're now ready for the next stage of the forcing process. Act now, and in less than a month, you can be enjoying a leafy luxury that's normally expensive to buy. You might even get a second harvest.

1 POT UP THE ROOTS
Plant several stored roots into a large pot, leaving the trimmed tops above the surface of the soil.

2 BLOCK OUT THE LIGHT
Cover the pot with another the same size, but block the drainage holes to exclude light from the roots.

3 GROW ON INDOORS
Grow the roots indoors at a temperature of 10°C (50°F) for 3–4 weeks. Water only in the dark.

4 HARVEST
After harvesting the leaves, water and re-cover the roots with the pot. They may crop again.

SOW

PEAS

WINTER SALAD CROP

WITLOOF CHICORY

NEW YEAR PEAS

HARVEST: **MAY–JUN**

If you live in a mild area, hardy peas can still be sown directly outside. In colder regions, sow them under cover for planting out in spring.

'DOUCE PROVENCE'
This is a high yield, dwarf variety that produces masses of sweet tasting peas. It only requires support in exposed sites.

'FELTHAM FIRST'
Very hardy, this dwarf variety gives an early crop of 10cm (4in) long green pods, packed with large peas. It is suitable for containers.

'METEOR'
Dwarf but highly productive, this variety produces abundant small pods, filled with fine-tasting peas. Grows well on exposed sites.

WINTER SALAD

If you have space in an unheated greenhouse or beneath a cold frame, you still have time to sow hardy oriental salad leaves, such as mizuna and mustard, for an early cut-and-come-again crop. Sow 1cm (½in) deep, in trenches 10–15cm (4–6in) wide, directly in the soil. You can also sow into large pots and bring them under cover. Harvest the young plants after a few weeks, although they may take some time to re-grow.

HARVEST: **ALL YEAR**

December: what to plant

PICK GARDEN NUTS

HARVEST: **SEP–OCT**

If you have space in your garden for a small apple tree, you could plant a cobnut instead. Depending on variety, you may need two for pollination.

'COSFORD'
This variety produces a heavy crop of thin-shelled, sweet-tasting nuts that are easy to crack open.

'KENTISH COB'
A self-fertile variety, so you only need one plant. It bears delicious, large nuts in late summer.

'RED FILBERT'
This red-leaved variety produces masses of tasty, red-shelled nuts. It is an attractive garden shrub.

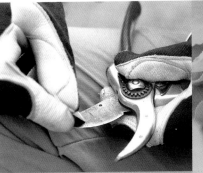

CARE FOR TOOLS

APRICOTS

COBNUTS

PLANT

TIMELY TOOL CARE

Finding time to maintain your gardening tools is difficult in the growing season, so make use of the relative lull now to lavish some care on them. Use a wire brush to remove mud from metal tools, and rub them with an oily cloth to prevent rust. Clean the blades of cutting tools, such as secateurs and loppers, with wire wool and sharpen them. Replace any blades that are damaged.

TREE PLANTING

Despite seeming tender, apricots can be planted from now until March, if the soil isn't frozen. To help protect the early blossom from frost and to ripen the fruit, pick a warm position against a south-facing wall. Add compost to the soil, and plant the tree to the same depth as it was in the nursery. Firm the soil and water-in well.

HARVEST: **JUL–AUG**

December: what to harvest

WINTER KALE

Kale is a useful ally among winter vegetables, and can be relied upon to tough-out almost any winter weather. It's a particularly good crop for smaller gardens because, although the plants are quite large and grow all summer, the leaves can be picked a few at a time, all the way through winter. If the weather turns really bad, such as heavy snowfall, harvest the best leaves and freeze them until needed. Even if your plants are damaged, leave them to recover and they may produce new leaves and shoots.

LAST OF THE CELERY

Able to withstand light frosts, trench celery is hardier than self-blanching types, and can be harvested through winter. As an extra precaution, give it a protective mulch of straw to keep it at its best. Lift earthed-up plants with a fork, or cut those blanched using collars right at the base, as required. Cut stems can be kept somewhere cool, stored in plastic bags, but whole plants are best left growing in the ground until needed.

HARVEST

POTATOES

KALE

PAK CHOI

TRENCH CELERY

LATE POTATOES

If you planted maincrop potatoes in midsummer, either in the ground or containers, you could well have tubers still to harvest. If the weather is cold, protect the remaining crop from frost by mulching with a thick layer of straw, or by moving containers under cover. Simply unearth the potatoes with a fork as required, and enjoy new potatoes at Christmas.

PAK CHOI NOW

Any late-summer sown pak choi, that were cloched or transplanted under cover in early autumn, should now be ready to harvest. Their fresh, mild leaves make a welcome contrast to the strong-flavoured, hardy winter brassicas. Pull up the plants whole or cut them off just above the soil, and they may well re-sprout.

SWEET WINTER GREENS

The first winter cabbages and endive, planted out in July, are ready to cut. If you have other vegetables to pick as well, leave a few cabbages growing for later. After a few hard frosts, their leaves become deliciously sweet, and are a real highlight of the season. To harvest, pull up the whole plant, and cut away the stem and any damaged outer foliage, to leave the firm green heart. While growing, these cabbages make handsome garden features, especially when they're dusted with crisp winter frost.

TASTY SPROUTS

Love or hate them, there's no denying that Brussels sprouts give a good winter crop. If you began sowing a succession of sprout varieties in February, then you'll be picking them from now until spring. Harvest the lower sprouts first, twisting them with your fingers, and work your way up the stem. Don't miss the leafy tops.

WINTER CABBAGE & ENDIVE

BRUSSELS SPROUTS

LEEKS

LIFT YOUR LEEKS

Mid- and late-season leeks, sown in spring, are ready to lift. Unearth them using a fork to prevent damaging the stems; the small roots grip fast.

'KING RICHARD'
Although this is an early variety, it stands until December in milder areas. It doesn't need earthing-up and is suitable for growing in pots.

'MUSSELBURGH'
This is a reliable, tasty variety that produces a heavy crop of strong, thick stems. It tolerates cold very well, and is good for exposed sites.

'TOLEDO'
A very hardy, late-season variety, it produces long tasty stems and resists bolting. The harvested leeks also store well if heeled in.

DON'T FORGET

If a spell of very cold weather is forecast, mulch any root crops still in the ground with thick straw. This stops the soil freezing, so they can still be dug up.

Storing vegetables

By using traditional storage techniques, you can look forward to home-grown vegetables throughout winter, anything from stacks of potatoes to a few prized squash. Some root crops can be left in the soil in mild areas, but most other vegetables should be harvested and stored. The important point is to keep them fresh, and to protect them from frosts, weather damage, and hungry insects and animals.

Roots in boxes

If you have space available in a cool, frost-free place, such as a shed, cellar, or garage, then try storing smaller root vegetables in boxes filled with light soil or sand. The method is simple and it keeps roots firm and fresh right through winter. Carrots, beetroot, turnips, celeriac, and parsnips can all be stored like this. You can fit several layers into a single box, which is ideal if you have only limited space indoors.

Whichever roots you store, lift them carefully, if possible when the soil is reasonably dry. If the roots are wet, lay them out on newspaper to dry fully and then brush off loose soil. Check each one, and store only crops that are disease-free and undamaged.

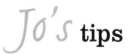

Jo's tips

The larger the root, the longer it will keep, so when storing in sand-filled boxes, pack the biggest specimens in the bottom layers and the smallest ones at the top.

Not all root crops keep well when lifted. Jerusalem artichokes and salsify lose their flavour and dry out once harvested.

1 REMOVE LEAVES
Remove all foliage before storing. Cut off carrot leaves 1cm (½in) above the roots and twist off the leaves of other vegetables with your hands, leaving a short tuft of stems at the top.

2 PREPARE YOUR BOX
Find a cardboard or wooden box that is wide and fairly shallow. Line it with newspaper if there are any gaps. Cover the base with a layer of light soil or sand about 2.5cm (1in) thick.

3 ARRANGE THE ROOTS
Place the first layer of roots with care to make maximum use of the space without one root touching another. Contact between them could allow rot to spread through the box.

4 LAYER THEM UP
Once the first layer is complete, cover it with at least 2.5cm (1in) of light soil or sand. Repeat the whole process until the box is full. Store in a dry, frost- and rodent-free place.

Clamping

This traditional method is ideal for storing large quantities of root crops, and involves piling them in a heap and insulating them with layers of straw. Providing the clamp can be kept dry, crops can be stored this way indoors or out. Stored vegetables must be dry, clean and undamaged, so check them thoroughly first. Outdoor clamps are prone to rodent attack, so watch for signs of disturbance, and set traps if need be. When emptying the clamp, take roots from one end only and carefully replace the layers once you have removed what you need.

1 LAY THE BASE
Spread a 20cm (8in) deep bed of straw on the soil in a sheltered spot, ideally against a wall. Arrange the roots on top to make a tapering heap that is a maximum 60cm (2ft) high.

2 PROVIDE INSULATION
Pack the same thickness of dry straw over the entire heap. If your clamp is indoors you can just cover it with hessian sacking or horticultural fleece weighed down at the edges.

3 ALL-WEATHER PROTECTION
Cover your outdoor clamp with a further layer of soil, about 15cm (6in) thick, to provide extra protection against cold and wet. Pack soil onto the straw from the base upwards.

4 ENSURE GOOD DRAINAGE
Soggy soil will rot stored roots from the base, so improve drainage by digging a shallow ditch around the edge of the clamp, using the soil to finish covering the top of the heap.

TRY THESE

Traditional methods can be used to store a wide range of crops, keeping them fresh to use without taking up space in your refrigerator or freezer.

Potatoes – Store maincrop varieties somewhere dry and frost-free in paper sacks, folded over to exclude light.

Bulbs – When dried, hang onions, shallots, and garlic in bunches somewhere cool, dry, and frost-free.

Squash – Once cured store squash and pumpkins under cover, on straw or shredded paper.

Beans – When the pods are dry and brittle, store the beans in screw-top jars indoors. Check them occasionally.

STORING VEGETABLES

Fruit: crop planner

Use this table to check when to sow, plant, prune, and harvest your fruit. Timings will vary for different climates so adjust them for your own site and conditions. Planting times refer to bare-root plants; container-grown shrubs and trees can be planted year-round.

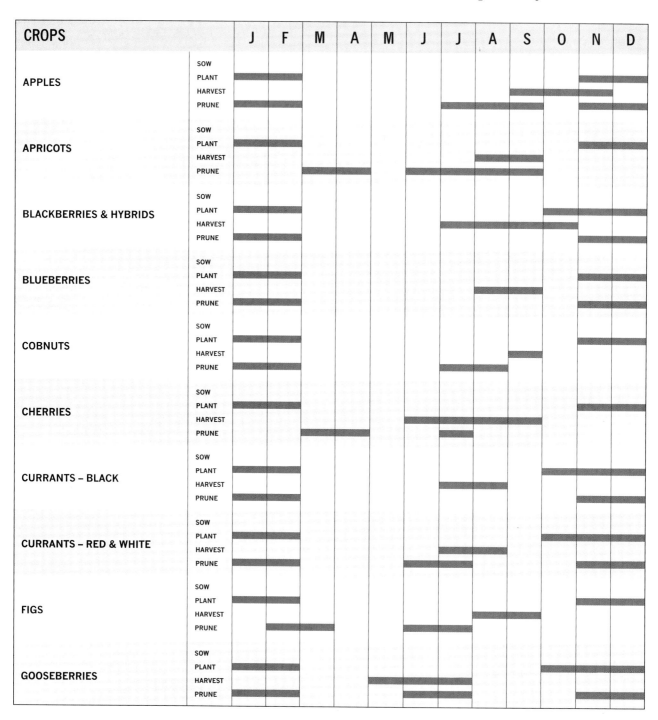

CROPS		J	F	M	A	M	J	J	A	S	O	N	D
APPLES	SOW												
	PLANT	■	■									■	■
	HARVEST									■	■	■	■
	PRUNE	■	■					■	■			■	■
APRICOTS	SOW												
	PLANT	■	■										
	HARVEST								■				
	PRUNE			■	■		■	■	■				
BLACKBERRIES & HYBRIDS	SOW												
	PLANT	■	■									■	■
	HARVEST							■	■	■			
	PRUNE											■	
BLUEBERRIES	SOW												
	PLANT	■	■									■	■
	HARVEST								■				
	PRUNE	■	■										
COBNUTS	SOW												
	PLANT	■	■									■	■
	HARVEST									■	■		
	PRUNE	■	■										
CHERRIES	SOW												
	PLANT	■	■									■	■
	HARVEST						■	■					
	PRUNE			■	■			■	■				
CURRANTS – BLACK	SOW												
	PLANT	■	■									■	■
	HARVEST							■	■				
	PRUNE	■						■				■	■
CURRANTS – RED & WHITE	SOW												
	PLANT	■	■									■	■
	HARVEST							■	■				
	PRUNE						■	■				■	■
FIGS	SOW												
	PLANT	■	■									■	■
	HARVEST								■	■			
	PRUNE		■	■			■						
GOOSEBERRIES	SOW												
	PLANT	■	■									■	■
	HARVEST					■	■	■					
	PRUNE						■	■				■	■

KEY

— SOWN, PLANTED, HARVESTED UNDER COVER
— SOWN, PLANTED, HARVESTED OUTDOORS

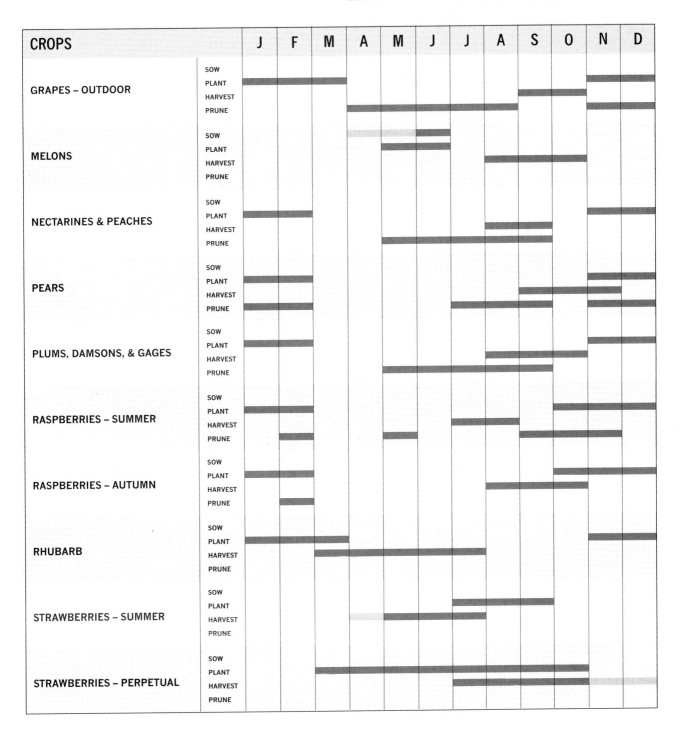

CROPS		J	F	M	A	M	J	J	A	S	O	N	D
GRAPES – OUTDOOR	SOW												
	PLANT	●	●	●								●	●
	HARVEST									●			
	PRUNE				●	●	●	●	●			●	●
MELONS	SOW				○	○	●						
	PLANT					●							
	HARVEST								●	●			
	PRUNE												
NECTARINES & PEACHES	SOW												
	PLANT	●	●										
	HARVEST								●				
	PRUNE					●	●	●					
PEARS	SOW												
	PLANT	●	●									●	●
	HARVEST									●	●		
	PRUNE	●	●					●	●			●	●
PLUMS, DAMSONS, & GAGES	SOW												
	PLANT	●	●									●	●
	HARVEST								●				
	PRUNE					●	●	●	●				
RASPBERRIES – SUMMER	SOW												
	PLANT	●	●	●								●	●
	HARVEST							●	●				
	PRUNE		○			●				●	●		
RASPBERRIES – AUTUMN	SOW												
	PLANT	●	●	●								●	●
	HARVEST								●	●	●		
	PRUNE		●										
RHUBARB	SOW												
	PLANT	●	●	●								●	●
	HARVEST			○	●	●	●						
	PRUNE												
STRAWBERRIES – SUMMER	SOW												
	PLANT							●	●				
	HARVEST				○	●	●	●					
	PRUNE												
STRAWBERRIES – PERPETUAL	SOW												
	PLANT			●	●	●	●	●	●	●	●		
	HARVEST							●	●	●	●		○
	PRUNE												

Vegetable: crop planner

Use this table to check when to sow, plant, prune, and harvest your vegetables. Timings will vary for different climates, so adjust them for your own site and conditions. For continuity, replace crops harvested in spring and summer with plants sown later.

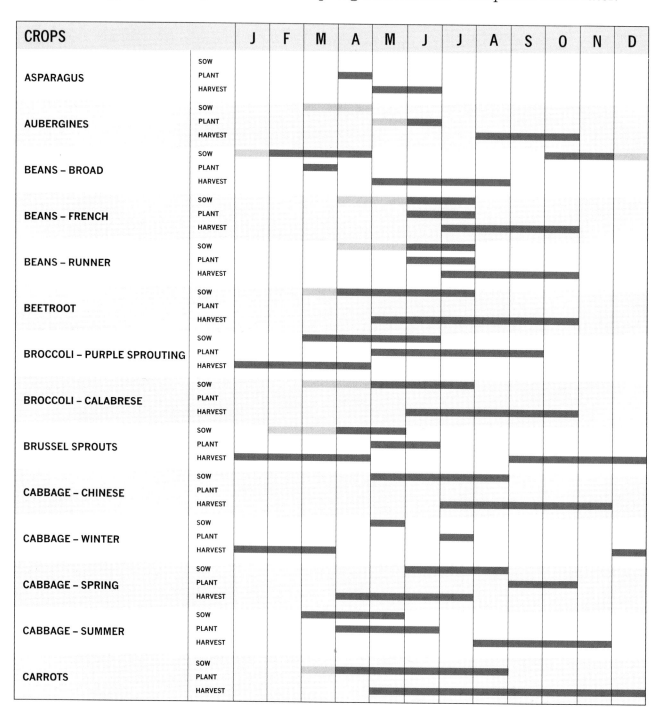

CROPS		J	F	M	A	M	J	J	A	S	O	N	D
ASPARAGUS	SOW												
	PLANT			■									
	HARVEST				■	■	■						
AUBERGINES	SOW			■									
	PLANT				■								
	HARVEST								■	■			
BEANS – BROAD	SOW	■	■								■	■	
	PLANT			■									
	HARVEST					■	■						
BEANS – FRENCH	SOW				■	■							
	PLANT						■	■					
	HARVEST							■	■	■			
BEANS – RUNNER	SOW				■	■							
	PLANT						■						
	HARVEST							■	■	■			
BEETROOT	SOW			■	■	■	■						
	PLANT												
	HARVEST					■	■	■	■	■	■		
BROCCOLI – PURPLE SPROUTING	SOW			■	■	■	■						
	PLANT				■	■	■						
	HARVEST	■	■										
BROCCOLI – CALABRESE	SOW			■	■	■							
	PLANT												
	HARVEST							■	■	■			
BRUSSEL SPROUTS	SOW		■	■									
	PLANT						■						
	HARVEST	■									■	■	■
CABBAGE – CHINESE	SOW					■	■						
	PLANT												
	HARVEST							■	■	■			
CABBAGE – WINTER	SOW					■							
	PLANT						■	■					
	HARVEST	■	■	■									■
CABBAGE – SPRING	SOW							■	■				
	PLANT									■	■		
	HARVEST				■	■							
CABBAGE – SUMMER	SOW		■	■									
	PLANT			■	■								
	HARVEST									■	■	■	
CARROTS	SOW		■	■	■	■	■	■					
	PLANT												
	HARVEST				■	■	■	■	■	■	■	■	■

KEY		SOWN, PLANTED, HARVESTED UNDER COVER
		SOWN, PLANTED, HARVESTED OUTDOORS

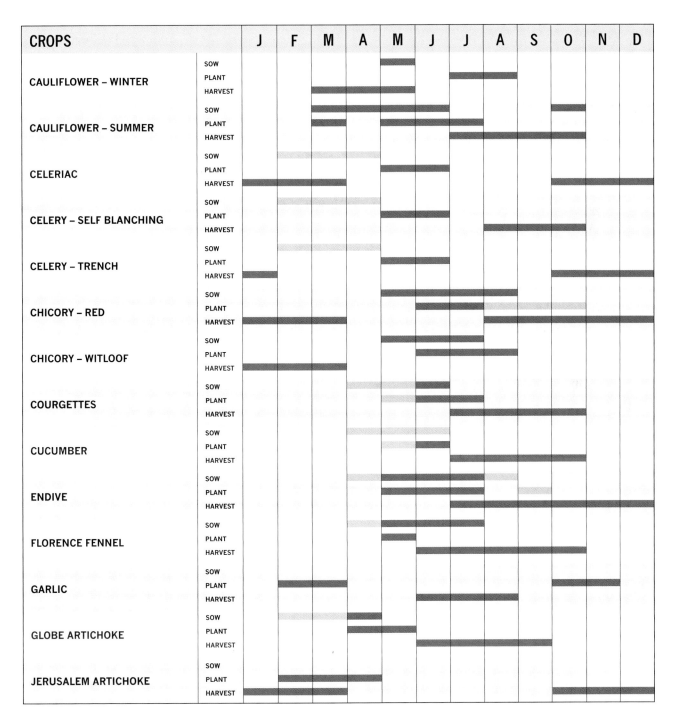

CROPS		J	F	M	A	M	J	J	A	S	O	N	D
CAULIFLOWER – WINTER	SOW					▬							
	PLANT							▬▬					
	HARVEST			▬▬▬									
CAULIFLOWER – SUMMER	SOW			▬▬		▬					▬		
	PLANT			▬▬		▬▬							
	HARVEST							▬▬▬▬					
CELERIAC	SOW		░░░░										
	PLANT					▬							
	HARVEST	▬										▬▬▬▬	
CELERY – SELF BLANCHING	SOW		░░░░										
	PLANT					▬							
	HARVEST								▬▬	▬			
CELERY – TRENCH	SOW		░░░░										
	PLANT					▬							
	HARVEST	▬										▬▬	
CHICORY – RED	SOW					▬							
	PLANT						▬▬		░░░				
	HARVEST	▬▬▬							▬▬			▬▬	
CHICORY – WITLOOF	SOW					▬▬							
	PLANT						▬						
	HARVEST	▬											
COURGETTES	SOW				░░		▬						
	PLANT						▬						
	HARVEST							▬▬▬▬					
CUCUMBER	SOW				░░░								
	PLANT				░░	▬							
	HARVEST							▬▬▬▬					
ENDIVE	SOW					░░░	▬						
	PLANT					▬▬				░░			
	HARVEST							▬▬			▬▬▬		
FLORENCE FENNEL	SOW				░░	▬							
	PLANT					▬							
	HARVEST						▬▬▬▬						
GARLIC	SOW												
	PLANT		▬▬▬								▬▬		
	HARVEST						▬▬▬						
GLOBE ARTICHOKE	SOW		░░░										
	PLANT				▬▬								
	HARVEST						▬▬▬						
JERUSALEM ARTICHOKE	SOW												
	PLANT		▬▬▬		▬							▬▬	
	HARVEST	▬▬▬										▬▬▬	

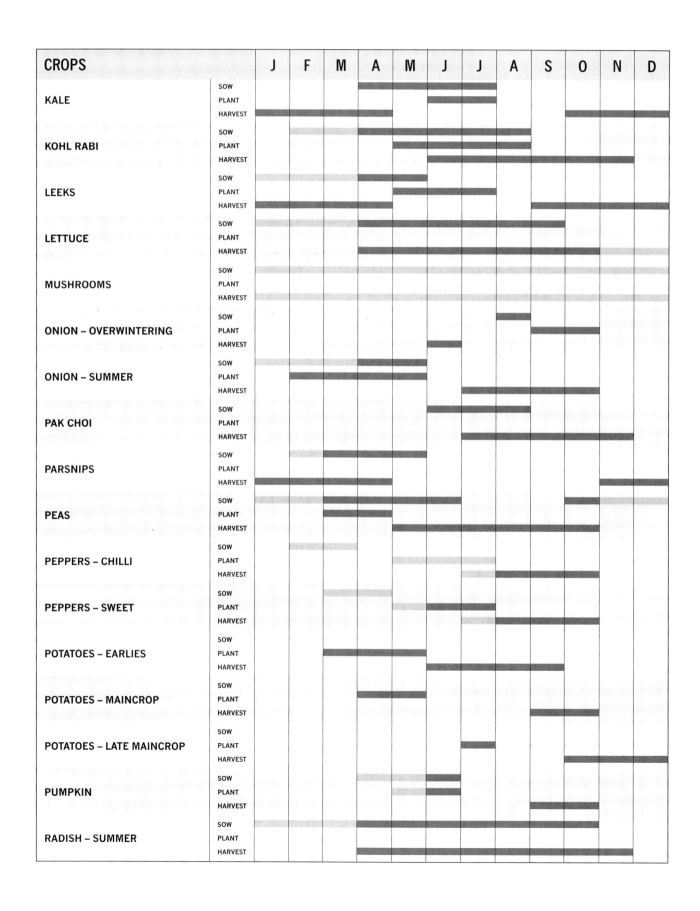

CROPS		J	F	M	A	M	J	J	A	S	O	N	D
KALE	SOW												
	PLANT												
	HARVEST												
KOHL RABI	SOW												
	PLANT												
	HARVEST												
LEEKS	SOW												
	PLANT												
	HARVEST												
LETTUCE	SOW												
	PLANT												
	HARVEST												
MUSHROOMS	SOW												
	PLANT												
	HARVEST												
ONION – OVERWINTERING	SOW												
	PLANT												
	HARVEST												
ONION – SUMMER	SOW												
	PLANT												
	HARVEST												
PAK CHOI	SOW												
	PLANT												
	HARVEST												
PARSNIPS	SOW												
	PLANT												
	HARVEST												
PEAS	SOW												
	PLANT												
	HARVEST												
PEPPERS – CHILLI	SOW												
	PLANT												
	HARVEST												
PEPPERS – SWEET	SOW												
	PLANT												
	HARVEST												
POTATOES – EARLIES	SOW												
	PLANT												
	HARVEST												
POTATOES – MAINCROP	SOW												
	PLANT												
	HARVEST												
POTATOES – LATE MAINCROP	SOW												
	PLANT												
	HARVEST												
PUMPKIN	SOW												
	PLANT												
	HARVEST												
RADISH – SUMMER	SOW												
	PLANT												
	HARVEST												

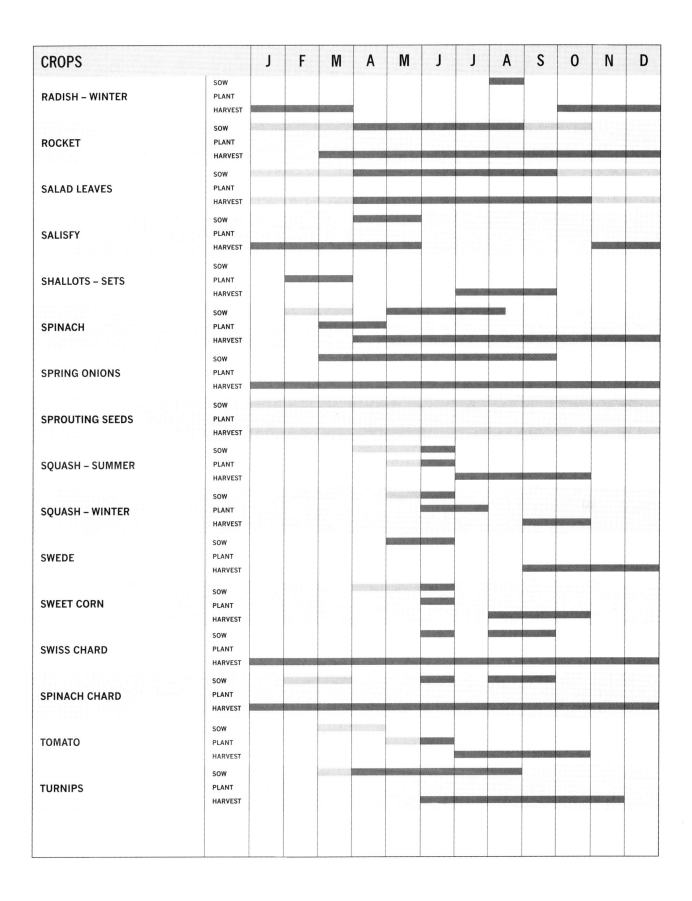

CROPS		J	F	M	A	M	J	J	A	S	O	N	D
RADISH – WINTER	SOW								▬				
	PLANT										▬		
	HARVEST	▬	▬	▬									
ROCKET	SOW	▬	▬	▬	▬	▬	▬	▬	▬	▬			
	PLANT												
	HARVEST			▬	▬	▬	▬	▬	▬	▬	▬	▬	▬
SALAD LEAVES	SOW	▬	▬	▬	▬	▬	▬	▬	▬	▬			
	PLANT												
	HARVEST	▬	▬	▬	▬	▬	▬	▬	▬	▬	▬		
SALISFY	SOW				▬	▬							
	PLANT												
	HARVEST	▬										▬	▬
SHALLOTS – SETS	SOW												
	PLANT		▬	▬									
	HARVEST							▬	▬				
SPINACH	SOW		▬	▬		▬	▬	▬					
	PLANT			▬	▬								
	HARVEST				▬	▬	▬	▬	▬	▬	▬	▬	▬
SPRING ONIONS	SOW			▬	▬	▬	▬	▬					
	PLANT												
	HARVEST	▬	▬	▬	▬	▬	▬	▬	▬	▬	▬	▬	▬
SPROUTING SEEDS	SOW	▬	▬	▬	▬	▬	▬	▬	▬	▬	▬	▬	▬
	PLANT												
	HARVEST	▬	▬	▬	▬	▬	▬	▬	▬	▬	▬	▬	▬
SQUASH – SUMMER	SOW				▬		▬						
	PLANT					▬							
	HARVEST							▬	▬	▬	▬		
SQUASH – WINTER	SOW					▬	▬						
	PLANT						▬						
	HARVEST									▬	▬		
SWEDE	SOW					▬	▬						
	PLANT												
	HARVEST									▬	▬	▬	
SWEET CORN	SOW					▬	▬						
	PLANT						▬						
	HARVEST								▬	▬	▬		
SWISS CHARD	SOW						▬		▬	▬			
	PLANT												
	HARVEST	▬	▬	▬	▬	▬	▬	▬	▬	▬	▬	▬	▬
SPINACH CHARD	SOW		▬	▬			▬		▬	▬			
	PLANT												
	HARVEST	▬	▬	▬	▬	▬	▬	▬	▬	▬	▬	▬	▬
TOMATO	SOW				▬	▬							
	PLANT					▬	▬						
	HARVEST								▬	▬	▬	▬	
TURNIPS	SOW				▬	▬	▬	▬	▬	▬			
	PLANT												
	HARVEST							▬	▬	▬	▬	▬	

Gardener's YEAR 2014

The publisher would like to thank the following for their kind permission to reproduce their photographs:

(Key: a-above; b-below/bottom; c-centre; f-far; l-left; r-right; t-top)

4 GAP Photos: Jo Whitworth (r).
5 GAP Photos: Pat Tuson (c). Harpur Garden Library: Jerry Harpur (br). Photolibrary: Stephen Hamilton (t).
6 GAP Photos: Maxine Adcock (cl); Lynn Keddie (bl).
6-7 The Garden Collection: Nicola Stocken Tomkins, Clinton Lodge. 7 GAP Photos: Friedrich Strauss (tc).
8 GAP Photos: Lee Avison (tr); Geoff Kidd (cra). Photolibrary: Mark Winwood (tl).
9 GAP Photos: BIOS/Gilles Le Scanff & Joëlle-Caroline Mayer (b). Victoriana Nursery Gardens: (c).
10 GAP Photos: Elke Borkowski (r); Juliette Wade (l).
11 The Garden Collection: Nicola Stocken Tomkins, Designer: Karen Maskell HCFS 2002 (br). Photolibrary: Mark Bolton (l).
17 Mike Shackleton: (tc).
18 Photolibrary: Howard Rice (cl).
19 Alamy Images: Gary Curtis (bl).
21 GAP Photos: Michael King/Design: Deborah Bird (bl); Michael King/Design: Greenfield Primary School (br); Clive Nichols/Location: Chelsea 2001 (bc).
22 Photolibrary: Francois De Heel (tl).
23 Thompson & Morgan: (cl).
24 Dobies of Devon: (tl) (tc). iStockphoto.com: (cl). Photolibrary: Michael Howes (bl). Thompson & Morgan: (tr).
27 Corbis: Paul Taylor (cr). GAP Photos: Lee Avison (cl).
28 Corbis: Ocean (bl/tatsoi). GAP Photos: Jonathan Buckley, Design: Sarah Raven (c).
29 Corbis: amanaimages (fcr); photocuisine (br). GAP Photos: Juliette Wade (cl). Photolibrary: Jo Whitworth (cr).
32 GAP Photos: Abby Rex (tr).
33 Alamy Images: Brian Hoffman (tl). The Garden Collection: Torie Chugg (tc). Garden World Images: MAP/Alain Guerrier (tr).
38 Garden World Images: Juliette Spears (fcl). Photolibrary: Howard Rice (fcr).
39 Thompson & Morgan: (c).
41 Corbis: Image Source (crb); Imagemore Co., Ltd. (cra); Helmut Meyer zur Capellen (br); Hein van den Heuvel (cr).
42 Corbis: Bill Barksdale/AgStock Images (bl); Radius Images (bc). GAP Photos: John Glover (fbl). Photolibrary: Maxine Adcock (tl). Victoriana Nursery Gardens: (cl).
43 GAP Photos: FhF Greenmedia (bc).
47 Photolibrary: Botanica (tr); Michael Howes (bl/slug pellets).
48 Photolibrary: Joshua McCullough (tl).
49 Corbis: Image Source (tr); Photolibrary (cl).
52 Photoshot: (cr/salsify). Suttons Seeds: (bl).
60 Corbis: Klaus Hackenberg (br).
63 Chauney Dunford: (crb). FLPA: Jef Meul/FN/Minden (cra); Martin B Withers (cr).
64 Getty Images: Michael Grimm (tr).

66 Photolibrary: Francesca Yorke (tl). www.dtbrownseeds.co.uk: (fcl) (cr).
67 Photolibrary: Maxine Adcock (tc).
71 Royal Horticultural Society, Wisley: (tr).
72 Corbis: image100 (tl); Ocean (bl).
73 Thompson & Morgan: (bc).
75 Marianne Majerus Garden Images: Marianne Majerus/The Old Rectory, Sudborough (l). Thompson & Morgan: (br).
76 Mr Fothergill's Seeds: (tr).
78 FLPA: Nigel Cattlin (br). naturepl.com: Gary K. Smith (bl). Photoshot: (cl).
79 Blackmoor Nurseries: (cl).
80 Photolibrary: Photos Lamontagne (tr).
82 Corbis: Wally Eberhart/Visuals Unlimited (fcr); Klaus Hackenberg (cl).
83 Corbis: Henglein and Steets/cultura (cr). GAP Photos: Jonathan Buckley (tr). Thompson & Morgan: (c). www.dtbrownseeds.co.uk: (tc/sunburst).
85 Garden World Images: Rita Coates (bl).
87 Marshalls Seeds: (tl). Suttons Seeds: (ftl). Thompson & Morgan: (ftr).
88 FLPA: Nigel Cattlin (tr).
91 Corbis: AgStock Images (cl); Emma Shervington (tr).
92 Photolibrary: Joshua Mccullough (ca); Photos Lamontagne (cra). 93 Photolibrary: Sally Reed (cr); Carol Sharp (br); Gary K Smith (crb).
95 Blackmoor Nurseries: (tr/'fantasia'). Photolibrary: Paroli Galperti (cr).
96 Photolibrary: Michael Howes (tr).
98 Victoriana Nursery Gardens: (br).
101 GAP Photos: Maxine Adcock (l). 102 Suttons Seeds: (tc) (tr). www.dtbrownseeds.co.uk: (tl).
103 Photolibrary: Gavin Kingcome (br).
104 Alamy Images: David Chilvers (cr). Photolibrary: Mark Bolton (tl). Jo Whittingham: (cl).
105 Photolibrary: Botanica (tr).
107 Corbis: C.Murtin/photocuisine (cl); John Smith (c). Chauney Dunford: (br).
110 Esther Ripley: (cl) (bl).
111 Photolibrary: Martin Page (br). Esther Ripley: (c).
113 Photolibrary: Michael Howes (bl); Craig Roberts (cl).
114 GAP Photos: Elke Borkowski (bl); Jonathan Buckley, Design: Sarah Raven (r). iStockphoto.com: John Sigler (c). Marshalls Seeds: (br). Photolibrary: Michael Davis (fbr). Suttons Seeds: (fbl).
115 Photolibrary: Lynn Keddie (bl); Mark Winwood (tr). Photoshot: (cl/salsify).
118 Victoriana Nursery Gardens: (bl).
119 Dobies of Devon: (tc). GAP Photos: Victoria Firmston (tr). Mike Shackleton: (br).
120 Corbis: Ocean (cr/pak choi). Photolibrary: Juliette Wade (br).
121 Corbis: Kai Schwabe/Westend61 (cr). GAP Photos: Nicola Browne (tr); Keith Burdett (tl). Suttons Seeds: (bl) (bc). Thompson & Morgan: (fbl).

All other images © Dorling Kindersley
For further information see:
www.dkimages.com